Thailand Transformed: 1950-2012

"Is Thailand the Test Case?"

Culver S. Ladd, Ph.D.
Former Teacher International School of Bangkok
And Special lecturer, Payap University, Chiang Mai

AuthorHouse™
1663 Liberty Drive
Bloomington, IN 47403
www.authorhouse.com
Phone: 1-800-839-8640

© 2012 Culver S. Ladd, Ph.D. All rights reserved.

No part of this book may be reproduced, stored in a retrieval system, or transmitted by any means without the written permission of the author.

Published by AuthorHouse 5/15/2012

ISBN: 978-1-4685-4735-1 (e)
ISBN: 978-1-4685-4736-8 (hc)
ISBN: 978-1-4685-4737-5 (sc)

Library of Congress Control Number: 2012904458

Any people depicted in stock imagery provided by Thinkstock are models, and such images are being used for illustrative purposes only. Certain stock imagery © Thinkstock.

This book is printed on acid-free paper.

Because of the dynamic nature of the Internet, any web addresses or links contained in this book may have changed since publication and may no longer be valid. The views expressed in this work are solely those of the author and do not necessarily reflect the views of the publisher, and the publisher hereby disclaims any responsibility for them.

Chapter III – Is Thailand the Test Case?, *previously copyrighted, 10/2003, for an Association of Asian Studies Conference held at George Washington University, October 2003.*

Chapter XII – THAILAND: An On-Going Struggle for Democracy, *previously copyrighted July 27, 2010 before presentation at the Middle Atlantic Region/ Association of Asian Studies, Pennsylvania State University. October 21-23, 2010.*

Table of Contents

Chapter I – Introduction to Development in Thailand	1
A leap of Faith into Southeast Asia	5
Teaching American History in Thailand	9
How Bangkok and Chicago had Similarities	11
Escalating Change in Thailand with Research Investment	13
Chapter II – Yanhee Multi-Purpose River Project – Thailand	20
Thailand Struggles for Development	20
Royal Irrigation Department Leads in Request for Financing	21
Bureau of Reclamation Survey	23
International Bank Guidance and Financing	25
Measures of the Success of the IBRD Guidance	27
Why Is Thailand the Test Case?	29
Chapter III – Is Thailand the Test Case?	30
Thailand's Emergence on the World Scene in Asia	31
Defense Against Communism	31
Creating an Environment for Diversification	35
Participant Training Inventories	40
Thailand's Rapid Growth Linked to Prudent Policies	41
Problems of Political and Administrative Development	44
Creating Community	47
This Mysterious Oneness	48
All Things Considered – Thailand's New Order	49
People Power	50
How Do You Clean Up Corruption	51
Adjusting the Economy After the Crash	52
Conclusion	53

Chapter IV – A Return for University Development in Thailand	54
A Return to Survey Research	58
Monsoon Drainage Systems	59
Fresh Water for a Growing City	59
A Look at the Need for Steel	61
The USOM-Thailand Contract	61
Valves, and More Valves	62
Infant Food Study	63
Payap College Opens Its Doors	63
Chapter V – Funding the University's Development	65
Chapter VI – Thailand Stumbles, Recovers and Is Growing: Asia and the World Are Watching.	72
The 1997 Economic Crisis	72
Politics Spelled: Thai Rak Thai Party	74
Thailand's First Completed Parliamentary Term: Thaksin's Way	77
Opposition Grows	77
Thailand's Functioning Bureaucracy	79
Ministry of Energy	80
Ministry of Transportation	81
Ministry of Industry and Ministry of Agriculture	85
Ministry of Interior and the Defense Ministry	87
Thailand Plunges in Global Ratings	90
China and India Sign Treaty of Amity and Cooperation with ASEAN	90
Investment flows back and forth to Asia	91
Corporate Governance/Best Listed Firms	92
Finance and Property Restructuring	92

Chapter VII – The Land of Smiles is Back to Being the Land of Coups	94
Give Dialogue a Chance	102
Economic Development under Coup Leadership	103
Power Adjustments	105
Thailand Ranks 5th in Foreign Capital Inflows	106
Thailand's International Contracting	106
Proposed Expansion of Chinese-Thai Traditional Trade	107
Thailand and China Open Linkage Discussions	108
Thailand as an Export Driven Economy	109
Cross-Border Agreements are a Key for Growth	109
Iran Holds out Possibility of Gas Pipeline	110
Industry/Steel and Investment	111
TAGS Wins Mideast Contracts	112
The Changed Tide of Traditional River Know-How	112
Ancient Law of King Mangrai	114
Tsunami Created Awareness	114
Chapter VIII – Basic Education Policies	115
Islam in State Schools	116
Thailand's IT Potential	117
Nurses Training for Southern Provinces	117
Universities Hit by "Brain Drain"	117
Chapter IX – Constitution Drafting	119
Constitution Drafting Assembly Accepts the Draft	123
Referendum Endorses Thailand's 18th Constitution	123
Chapter X – Thailand's Political Drama	126
PAD Mass Protests Special Coverage	128
PAD Wrong to Block Airport	128

Chapter XI – Thailand's Rocky Road Ahead	130
Airlines seek redress for PAD actions	130
We need a PM we can trust	131
Thai Premier leans Right to Placate Bargain Factors That Put Him in Power	132
Rough Economic and Political Challenges	133
Pro-Thaksin Rallies Grow	133
The Dawning of New Realities	134
Conclusions on the Thai Developmental Model for Asia	135
Chapter XII – THAILAND: An On-Going Struggle for Democracy	138
Thailand's Supreme Court Confiscates B46.37bn from Thaksin	138
The Leaders of PAD and UDD	139
Academics Urge Political Talks	141
Use of force still an option for the army	142
PM meets with governors in red rallies	142
Not the same Silom anymore	142
Red shirts get 15 days in jail	143
PAD renews call for swift end to protests	143
New Thai violence kills 2, mars compromise moves	143
'Guilty' Seh Daeng faces dismissal, stripping of rank	144
Thailand sizzles as temperatures go through the roof	146
Put an end to this rebellion	147
Ultimatum passes as battles rage on in Bangkok	147
Government rules out talks unless rally ends	147
Violence erupts after red-shirt leaders surrender	147
Troops retake area around main protest site	148
New task force to return city to normal	149
Unsung heroes of Klong Toey repel red threat	150

In devastated Bangkok, residents join city workers in cleanup efforts	150
Governors and Police Chiefs in NE provinces removed	151
Safety concerns hang over city's 'new beginning'	151
DSI seeks 20 new warrants for terrorism	152
Thailand's Reform Efforts	152
PM plans to wait until dust settles	152
Chuan urges police reform	153
Abhisit & Co. survive but parliament takes a drubbing	153
Abhisit: Corruption root of problems	153
Police reform panel chief appointed	154
Conclusions on the Struggle for Democracy	154
Human Rights and Social Justice in Asia	156
Thailand's Human Rights & Social Justice Issues	158
Bangkok Metropolitan Administration is Building Flood Drainage Tunnels Under the City	159
Expanding Thai Industrial Development	160
Infrastructure Needs	161
Just a Note on Thai Industrial Development	162
Critical Thai Civil Rights Issues	162
Urgent Need for Land Reforms	163
Need for Truth and Reconciliation	164
Samut Sakhon Province Coal-Mining Conflicts	165
His Majesty the King Urges Compassion	165
Tormenting Issues Afflicting Thai Society	166
Cambodia's Khao Preah Vihear Temple	167
Chapter XIII – Moving Toward a Democratic Election	170
From The Democratic Party's Perspective	170
Democrat Party launches Thailand Reform Plan	171
Government Enters Its Final Week	172

Peoples Alliance for Democracy Asks EC to Dissolve Pheu Thai Party	173
Democrat Party Offers Banned Politicians Amnesty	174
From the Puea Thai Party Perspective	174
Criteria for Leadership	177
Constitution Court Approves Election-Related Bills	178
On the Campaign Trail	180
International Media Takes Notice of the Thai Election	181
Southern Thailand Arena of Conflict	182
Thailand's General Election	182
Democrats Seek P.T. Dissolution	184
Election Commission Acts	185
Yingluck Shinawatra: Sister Act	186
Royal Decree Endorsement	187
Conclusions on the Struggle for Democracy in Thailand	188
How Disaster is Contributing to Reconciliation.	189
Index	191

"Thailand, the Test Case"
As Viewed from
Between the legs of a Stool

By: Culver Sprogle Ladd. Ph.D.

Chapter I

Introduction to Development in Thailand

My advisor for the Masters Degree in 1963 at The American University, Dr. Harold H. Roth, said, "Mr. Ladd, you should teach!" Teach what and where?

And then, <u>Presbyterian Life</u> magazine advertised, "Bangkok Christian College needs teachers.[1] I had the answer!

Why was that an answer? It is fundamental to understand why I arrived at that decision then. Two factors were important: my Church background and the University of Maryland leadership roles I had played there. My pastor in Washington was a China-born mission kid, and Princeton Seminary classmate of the Chief of Presbyterian missionaries in Thailand. At Maryland I had created the first Campus

---

[1] *Presbyterian Life*, 1964: **Christian Volunteers in Thailand**. 26 Christian men or women needed for 1965 in church-related schools. Minimum age 18, Volunteer pays transportation; school provides living and stipend. Inquire air-mail Konrad Kingshill, CVT Administrator, Bangkok Christian College, Bangkok, Thailand.

Fund Drive with specific funding for World Universities Service Fund targeting Asian university libraries. Couple all of that with Korean Conflict active duty Air Force assignments in Japan, recent work with the law firm of Covington & Burling, as Assistant Office Manager on law cases dealing with the Pakistan Water Delegation and its Indus River Basin hydropower developments and a law case that Dean Acheson argued in the World Court between Thailand and Cambodia on the temple of Khao Phra Vihar, and you can understand that I had an Asian interest.

After receiving the Masters Degree in Public Administration I headed to Harvard University for Summer School in July 1963. That was a very good change of pace, with classes in American Political Theory and Cultural Anthropology; very different from The American University at 19th and F Streets, N.W. However, I attended lectures in Honor of William Y. Elliott, who was retiring after 30 + years as head of the Department of Government and going to The American University, in Washington, D.C. I obviously was going the wrong direction!!

Dr. Roth was quite surprised to see me return in the Fall Term 1963. I was determined to have a class with Dr. Elliott and finally got one scheduled in the Spring Term 1964. That was one of the most important classes I ever enrolled in, a class in Political Theory. Our first class meeting was attended by 12 to 15 students and Dr. Elliott informed us of his requirements and that we would meet regularly. The second meeting was attended by six or maybe seven students. It seems that his requirement "…of at least 75 pages to begin to fully express yourself" surprised some at our first meeting.

Dr. Elliott suggested that each of us should sketch out some ideas of what we would write about and arrange to come to his office for an appointment in the next week. This was a very unique experience, as I was trying to build academic strength in Political Theory for Doctoral Comprehensives. My suggestions included Hobbes, Locke and other

British theorists. Elliott asked "why do you not suggest the French," and further "...do you read French?" To which I replied, "No, I do not read French." And of course he went on to comment how much better it is to read in the original language.

And now comes the guidance, "You might begin with a look at Jean Bodin, *Six Books of the Commonweale*, (1530-1596);and then of course read some of Baron Charles Montesquieu, in the *Spirit of the Laws*, (1689-1755), and read *Democracy in America*, written by Alexis de Tocqueville, (1805-1859)." He then suggested reading a bit and then sketching out what I might suggest as an outline and "...let's talk again." It was this kind of interacting in the teaching process that I had not experienced before. Here we were shaping a doctoral dissertation I would write twenty years later. The paper I wrote and delivered in the last class was titled: The Development of Constitutionalism. I think it exceeded the 75 page requirement, because these are the great thinkers who shaped and commented on the America we all know as so unique in world politics, and they did excite me.

During the summer of 1964 I was engaged in preparation for comprehensive examinations. On August 5, 1964 I was driving back to Washington from Harrisburg, Pennsylvania with several cousins when we heard President Lyndon B. Johnson announce that we had been attacked in the Gulf of Tonkin by Vietnamese ships. And I commented to those cousins, "Well I know what that means, I will be headed to South-East Asia very soon." During the Fall Term 1963 I had enrolled for my first course on the Main American University Campus on Massachusetts Avenue, N.W. a Seminar on International Relations taught by Dr. Ernest W. LeFever, an adjunct professor associated with Brookings Institution. He was planning to be in the Congo during some portion of our class so we worked to structure projects quickly when we first met. I wanted to do a paper on Thailand in Southeast Asia, and asked his advice on using the National War College library at Ft. McNair, D.C. He asked if I had credentials for admission and I said yes, I did have a military ID, and he said go ahead. That was a most fortuitous event because once I gained admission and told the librarians what I was studying, they deluged me with the latest articles on that subject. I have never had such treatment in any library since that visit in the fall of 1963.

The Virginia Quarterly Review, 1950-51 had a most amazing treatment of South east Asia, and particularly with regard to Thailand. Professor Amry Vandenbosch of the University of Kentucky wrote the article, *Thailand, the Test Case*. The essence of what he was saying was that **soft-power** was a valid approach to international relations. China and India are too large countries for the United States to make major socio-economic changes within them, whereas Thailand is between them and it is more possible to help them achieve those desired transformations! And, let both China and India watch those changes, and let them change themselves. Though Vandenbosch did not use the term *soft-power*, he did in fact define what it has come to be understood to accomplish in international relations. Now in the twenty-first century we can look back some fifty years and clearly see that the Thai transformations are contributing to both Chinese and Indian transformations as business and economic interactions are consistently occurring among these nation-states.

In the process of developing data for that paper on American Involvement in Thailand I was told of an adjunct professor who was coming to join the faculty of the School of International Service in the future, now heading Southeast Asian studies at the Foreign Service Institute of the State Department, a Dr. Kenneth P. Landon. I called upon him at the Institute in Arlington and got some first hand knowledge of Thailand politics. The next time I was to see Dr. Landon was in Bangkok, Thailand when he delivered a Lecture to the American

Chamber of Commerce in 1966 and he commented that students of his did sometimes disappear.

A leap of Faith into Southeast Asia

The Tonkin Gulf Resolution of August 8, 1964 set my course of action for Thailand, I knew from experience in Japan, how the Korean Conflict had importantly helped Japanese post war development and knew that something similar was to affect Thailand. During the fall term I supported myself doing survey research for the firm Mendota Research of New Jersey interviewing physicians on their use of various pharmaceuticals, this was my first experience with survey research methodologies. Once I finished a draft Political Science paper for Dr. Edgar Robinson, political theory reader at the School of Public Affairs, and the pending 1964 Election votes were cast I was ready to depart for Thailand. I left Washington after the 15th of November 1964 by military air to Spokane, Washington, by train down to Seattle and by Pan Am flight to Honolulu for shopping and some beach time. Then I caught Pan Am flight #1 to Bangkok via Tokyo and Hong Kong, arriving at the American Club on Wireless Road at 2:30am, Sunday morning, November 22, 1964.

When one de-planes at Don Muang Airport, Bangkok and that heat and humidity strikes you for the first time, you suddenly know you are in the tropics: Bangkok is known to be the hottest city in the world, and there are those occasions when you know that is true! However, there are those other occasions after a three hour monsoon downpour is ended and the evening breezes begin and it is quite pleasant even in June and July. Now, in the 21st Century Bangkok has ability to adjust easily, whereas in 1964 I arrived just before the first wave of changes arrived and it was stifling. The first change I was expecting was hydropower from the Yanhee Dam on the River Ping; it did not arrive until late December.

My research had shown me what was transpiring in Thailand, Jorgenson & Jorgenson were there (from 14th Street between F & G Streets above the Hot Shoppes), a communications engineering firm placing repeater antennae on mountain tops to carry signals from Bangkok studios to peasant villages in Thailand's mountain valleys. It was more than a dozen years since Vandenbosch had posed his thesis on Thai development, and much development had been occurring. After a couple hours of sleep I was up and off to Church, at Wattana Chapel on Soi 19, Sukhumvit Road. However, I missed the English language service and sat through a Thai Service and then inquired about other services that same day. The organist spoke perfect English and gave me complete details and offered to drive me back to the American Club after the students were release to go home with their parents.

Now comes my introduction to education in polite "Thai Society." As I sat on the porch of the administration building of Wattana Wittaya Academy, a Presbyterian missionary school for girls founded in 1874, students came forward and knelt with their head on their hands at the foot of their teacher, who then dismissed them to return home with their parents. This is the first school for girls outside of the Palace grounds in Thailand and it is the premier preparatory school for Thai women. For an American this was quite an introduction to Thailand as it truly educates its younger generation. All the teachers I saw that day were Thai women, foreign women did not appear in this ceremony of respect and honor, *teaching an ethic of politeness.*

The organist drove me back to the American Club where I was met by Thai faculty people who had studied in the States. We had lunch together and I made the mistake of eating a salad in Bangkok. For the next two months I was sick, until I was Hospitalized in February at the Seventh Day Adventists Hospital for nearly three weeks and bedridden for two months with Acute Glomerulonephritis, a childhood disease that killed Britt Hadden, co-founder of Time Magazine in 1929.

I survived because Penicillin and Aeromyasin had been invented and were available in Thailand.

Though I ws sick constantly losing weight with diarrhea and occasional vomiting, I did keep busy. I attended church at Fourth Church that first evening and met with Dr. Horace Ryburn, head of Presbyterian missions in Thailand and arranged to come into his office the next morning. The next morning I met with Konrad Kingshill the author of the ad that brought me to Thailand to teach. His comment was: "Look across the street, we are tearing it down, why did you not write, I would have told you to come next year." What was happening across the street was actually changing the face of Thailand, more about that later.

Konrad did have a suggestion, "Go to IIE (Institute of International Education) up the street, and ask them for some ideas on places to teach." And so I left and walked a half mile or so to IIE offices and the director, Dr. John Brohm was out of town and his wife suggested I go to the International School of Bangkok. I soon found my way to Soi 15, Sukhumvit Road and the International School of Bangkok, (ISB). Yes, they were interested, and if I would call and they had a need, I would be teaching. A couple of mornings later I was teaching JoAnne Hankins class on Asian Studies. Substitute teaching was fun and yet I was told I should visit Chiang Mai in north Thailand. So early in December I took the train to Chiang Mai and sought out John Hamlin, principal of Thailand Theological Seminary, and inquired about anthropological digs in north Thailand, which was a jump back to my Cultural Anthropology class at Harvard. He did not know of any in the north, but only in the far northeast of Thailand. On my rented motorcycle I explored Chiang Mai and its mountain top temple of Doi Sutep. Sunday I was at first church on the Ping River and met an American lady with a broad brimmed hat, who suggested I come home with her and meet "the doctor." Charlotte McDaniel was the first

American to invite me into their home to meet Dr. Edwin McDaniel surgeon and medical missionary. They were close friends of mine all of their lives, and Chiang Mai has become one of those special places in Southeast Asia.

That was a very fine introduction to some of the heartland of Thailand, and its people, some of whom live in the mountain-tops. There are many peoples in Thailand, unified by a monarchy and held together with deep cultural roots that give the society a politeness that is refreshing in a world of brashness. And so I returned to Bangkok and a teaching assignment that ebbed-and-flowed depending on who was ill. In late December all of Bangkok electric power companies merged their activities with the new flow of yanhee power coming in and nightly power outages ceased. A new 220 volt system was adopted in exchange for the 110 volt system and economics was credited with that necessity. The inherent dangers of that conversion have never been discussed. At about that same time, weather changed and I caught cold, and that increased my sickness, such that by the end of January 1965 I was swelling and unable to get my shoes on easily. Since I knew the chief pharmacist at the embassy medical unit, I call on them and they took samples of blood. Jess Day called and invited me to supper at their home and informed me I needed immediate medical help. He arranged my entry into the 7th day Adventist hospital where Dr. Kenneth D. Doran saved my life.

Those teachers at ISB spearheaded by Mrs. Bernice Scheible and her husband inquired and arranged for me to share a house with a young officer near their home. Lt. Oscar Chase, invited me to share his house and arranged for a steady supply of good food, and for two months I was bed-ridden. Mid-April I was cleared by Dr. Doran to get up and teach, and I returned to ISB full time replacing a dismissed teacher of American History and United States Government. I often say, I never quit teaching from then until 2001, which is true except for some time in classes for the advanced degrees; so thankful to be alive and productive.

Teaching American History in Thailand

This was a most unique experience if you teach our history from discovery to modern times in a continuous flow in a single year in a developing country like Thailand was in 1965-67. It crystallizes aspects of our process of development that are essentially needed for Thailand's development too. The inflow of educated immigrants into America led it to change and develop: in essence education for all citizens means fundamental changes can occur as they employ their new knowledge in life's processes. European immigrants were all educated peoples, many coming for religious freedom but all with skills needed in those colonies. Pennsylvania was founded by Germans with steel-making skills that led to wagon production that opened the roads to transport and stimulated commerce among the colonies. The flow of ideas from Scotland and England led to the control of steam for powering vessels which further stimulated ocean commerce. Steel making in America was spurred by Andrew Carnegie, an immigrant Scotsman.

The International School of Bangkok was a unique school for Americans abroad often dependent schools are located on military bases and closely associated with the American governmental functions. ISB is a Thai-entity with a multi-national board of directors. The superintendent in 1964, was Dr. Carlisle Kramer, (importantly for me he was a reserve colonel in the USAFR), and the Principal of the Senior High School was Mr. Shelton Marlow, who cautioned me, "...never walk into class without full preparation ahead of time." These men knew me and my credentials including the recent Masters Degree in Public Administration. Based on that background I was teaching American History and in the second year I added United States Governments. Both summers, 1965 and 1966 I taught Summer School and in addition with Col. Kramer's help I won orders for active duty training with the United States Air Force. The first assignment was in August 1965 at Clark Air Force Base in the Philippines, where I wrote a staff study on the subversive threats within the Philippines. The second two week assignment in 1966 was at Headquarters MACTHAI, in Bangkok, developing guidelines for Americans now coming in increasing numbers into the Thai Society as the V-N War intensified.

In late 1965 I heard that the University of Maryland was planning to open classes in Thailand and I wrote College Park and inquired if that was true. Dr. Ray Ehrensberger answered that yes, they would be opening classes in 1966, and I would be interviewed for a position. Shortly after that Dr.Joseph Dellen from the Tokyo office of UMUC-Asia visited me at ISB and I was selected to teach in the first semester April 1966. Maryland classes begin at 7 PM and extend to 10 PM. That was a three hour lecture twice a week for a three credit course in University College. From the teacher's perspective, preparing for six hours of lecture each week is **heavy work.** Now my assignments were beginning with class at 7:30 AM until 2:30 PM at the ISB and from 7PM to 10 PM usually on Tuesdays and Thursdays for the University of Maryland at the ISB building.

Fortunately, I lived on Soi 21, Soi Asoke, a short few blocks from ISB, and the evening classes were escorted by staff cars of the US Army. I had received the certification letter form the University College offices in College Park, Maryland that I was certified to teach: Publi Administration; Business Enterprise; Personnel Management I & II; and Organization and Management Theory. The first class I was to teach was Business Enterprise and all materials had been sent to me and I was fully briefed and ready for that class. The first evening Dr. Joseph Mabbett arrived by staff car and picked me up at my resident in Soi Asoke, and we drove to ISB and discussed how we would begin. Joe said "…go in and begin," and he went next door and opened his class. A University College Term is two months long, thus we teach five two-month terms each year. Dr. Mabbett was a full-timer for University College and he traveled to a different country site each term, ending in Tokyo at the end of the five term cycle; I was local hire as was true for the ISB teaching assignment as well.

Let us stop and reflect a moment on Thailand in 1966-67 with recent hydro-power coming on line from Yanhee Dam on the Ping River in western Thailand; more power was available but lines had to be strung for increase power loads. The International School of Bangkok was one of the most modern buildings in Bangkok yet it lacked air conditioning. It also lacked screens on the windows. That was fine in the early morning, and school was dismissed shortly after noon; evening classes posed a very different story. Each classroom had two ceiling fans one for the students to cluster under and one for the lecturer. The lights attracted the mosquitoes and other flying insects which always seemed to fly into your open mouth. This was a challenging environment for both students and faculty.

How Bangkok and Chicago had Similarities

In the late 1950s and into 1960, the Presbyterian mission was asked by the Thai Government to sell property it owned on Sukhumvit Road for the Thais to construct a planetarium for educational purposes. The Presbyterians had planned to use that property for an institution of higher education, but the Government had consistently refused all such permission, even though the Presbyterians had developed a complete nation-wide system of schools for Thai students. The property was sold for a million dollars, and now Bangkok Christian College (K-12) was being rebuilt. BCC was founded for boys outside of Palace Schools in 1854, and was the cornerstone institution for such education in Thailand.

I arrived in 1964, after all plans had been made and engineering done for that reconstruction. The person doing this engineering is the real story here: Linne Tholin, the retired Chief Engineer for Chicago, Illinois had asked his Swedish Lutheran Church if they could use his skills, and they responded, no, but the Presbyterians might need them. When Linne arrived in Thailand in 1962 the tallest building in Thailand was five floors, because they sank into the soft soil. All drainage was with open sewers, called *klongs*, Bangkok had almost no modern facilities for housing, for transportation, or for industry: the pace of change was very slow.

Linne took soil samples and decided that the Bangkok soil situation on the Chao Phraya River was nearly identical to Chicago at the bottom of Lake Michigan. Bangkok Christian College needed pilings: 27 meter concrete reinforced steel pilings. When he started driving those pilings nearly ninety feet tall into the ground at BCC, Thai engineers stood aghast, never had they thought of such methodologies. Linne was introducing the very most modern methodology for Thailand's development: and I might add for all of East Asia, too!

While I was at Clark AFB in the Philippines in 1965 I was invited to attend the Commanding General's Briefing and heard that President Johnson was escalating involvement in V-N, and I was invited to stay on active duty and go to Vietnam. I declined and returned to ISB to complete a teaching contract. As a result of that escalation American personnel in Thailand began to increase markedly. Linne was consulted on the needs for additional office space for American agencies and the result was the first tall building in Thailand: the twenty-four storey Chokchai Building at Soi 26, Sukhumvit Road, completed in 1969. Everyone predicted it would fall over, but it has not done so. And then Thanpuying Chanut Piyaoui[2], a distinguished hotelier invested in the Dusit Thani Hotel at Silom Road and Rama IV Road, completed in 1970. These are the two founding ***tall buildings*** in Bangkok. In 2006 the

---

2   *BangkokPost.Com*, March 19, 2006, "Pioneering Lady of Thai Hospitality."

skyline is totally changed in metropolitan Bangkok, the tallest building now exceeds 84 floors and elevators and air conditioning are standard throughout the city.

A sidelight on this ***tall building*** event in Thailand is that China sent a delegation in 1972 for what was referred to as *ping-pong diplomacy* in Thailand with high ranking diplomats engaged in discussions on the V-N conflict, and they stood amazed at those buildings in Bangkok; China had none of those. The reports back to Chairman Mao and Deng Xiaoping may well have ignited China's determination to make changes itself.

Escalating Change in Thailand with Research Investment

When the fifth term for the classes at Maryland University (FED) ended May 30, 1966 I was scheduled to teach Summer School, but I also had some free time in the afternoons, and so logically I explored an opportunity to engage in survey research with Business Research Company, Ltd. (BRL). Dr. Frederic L. Ayer, research director invited me to come in and do some work with them. I had done some such research and thought this would be an interesting experience in understanding Thailand and its process of development.

The offices of BRL at 712/4 Sukhumvit Road, were newly built and *air-conditioned*. In mid-July 1966 that was pretty nice, and I was challenged to gather data on newspapers in Bangkok, Chinese as well as Thai and the English language publications like the Bangkok Post and The Nation. I was getting a feel of Thailand and its commercial activities. After my active duty with MACTHAI headquarters I returned to BRL and Dr. Ayer offered me a years assignment. I accepted and notified ISB I would not be returning. I was tasked with preparing <u>Studies on Thailand's Market Potential,</u> focusing on three areas: Edible Fats and Oils Industry in Thailand; The food Processing Industry in Thailand: The Rubber and Rubber Products Industry in Thailand; and The

Culver Ladd

Even in the 1970s, change was very slow. Typical shophouses were two or three storeys!

General Costs in the Operation of Industries in Thailand; contracted by the United Nations Economic Commission for Asia and the Far East (ECAFE), for presentation at the Asian Trade Fair seminars in November and December 1966.

This was an all consuming effort to gather data from published sources and confirm details with interviews of managers of processing plants across Bangkok and its outlying communities. Traditionally, Bangkok's residents had cooks who shopped three times daily for fresh food, refrigeration was unheard of. But now with electricity, change was possible, and as I said at that time:

> "As the nation of Thailand moves toward urbanization, industrialization, and the disruption of its traditional agrarian life, its population is gradually moving to accept new foods and new ways of buying, storing, and utilizing foods. It is out of this pattern of change that we see the coming growth of new important industry for the nation, an industry involved in and even dedicated to the processing of food in a healthful and convenient form for use of the many people now moving to live in cities.[3]

The contrast between traditional and modern plants was dramatic, e.g., I visited a Firestone Tyre & Rubber Co. (Thailand) Ltd. Plant outside of Bangkok which was in fact directly imported from the States, with all its safety devices and modern cafeteria facilities, and also a Chinese Tire plant with ***none of these facilities;*** an abattoir, where cultural beliefs determined duty assignments, i.e., moslem men did not deal with pigs, rather they butchered water buffalo or cattle, while Chinese men butchered pigs; I visited one of Thailand's first frozen seafood plants, where I was impressed by the care taken in the washing and freezing that they were doing for shipment to the West and Japan.

---

3   BUSINESS RESEARCH LTD., *Studies on Thailand's Market Potential*, October 1966, p. 20.

As I was writing this in 1966, shops were beginning to show refrigerators for sale, Thailand was beginning to make basic changes in daily living. Nothing is instantaneous, when it comes to cultural changes, they come in time as individuals decide to change. To give up shopping three times daily to buying food weekly is a dramatic personal change. For shop keepers to sell multiple items unrelated to each other as we know in mass marketing is another dramatic change. Many European countries still have shop next to shop selling individual items of produce: cheese shops, meat shops, vegetable shops, and bakery. Now in 2006, Bangkok, Chiang Mai and many other Thai cities have large mass markets. Central Department store has mass food markets and food courts with street vendors now inside preparing food in much cleaner and sanitary environments. In other words, sanitation is beginning to become important to Thai customers. The crowds in McDonald's and KFC's are also testimony to a desire for sanitary food preparation.

The next crisis I was to deal with was the Port of Bangkok, at Klong Toey, where ship traffic was backing up in the Gulf of Siam from four to six weeks of delays. That sort of delay causes shipping magnets to get ulcers. Of course the problem was American munitions shipments and re-transport to air force bases for loading and delivery to Vietnam. Thailand had never seen such ship traffic and stevedores quit work at sunset. The girls go aboard at dusk and work until daylight. Here the difficulty was changing whole working customs. My task was working between United Stevedoring Co., Ltd. And dockside managers. My colleague, from the International Executive Service Corps was a Mississippi River Barge company owner charged with opening the stevedore company's vision of the future with the possibility of managing the operations at the U.S. built port on the Gulf of Siam, being constructed at Sattahip. Ultimately we succeeded, and ships began to be off-loaded twenty-four hours daily, seven days a week, some from mid-stream sites by barges.

Esso Standard Thailand, Ltd. Needed an evaluation of their American slogan campaign, *"Put a Tiger in Your Tank"* for a Thai environment where tigers were a real fear for people both in rural villages and recent settlers in cities. I delighted in writing that study, and now in visiting Thailand I see Esso Tiger Plazas throughout the countryside. It has been a very successful brand-loyalty slogan. We did a study of menthol flavored lozenges for Bayer-Pharma (Thailand) Ltd. And could report from both household interviews and from panels of customers that they enjoyed those lozenges.

Dun and Bradstreet International asked if we would develop data on corporations applying for financing internationally. This is a very fundamental part of international financing of private enterprises. In essence are these applicants honest in what they say of their corporate structure. We developed measures of their corporations, actually measuring plants and offices and assessing their financial resources for evaluation.

The last project I worked on in 1967 before returning to the States was the design of the acceptability of the rice bagasse paper-making process for The Siam Kraft paper Co., Ltd. This effort involved working with management of stores and markets to evaluate their needs in Kraft paper containers. We were searching for convenient sizes and acceptability of paper products in their daily business. The design and field work were launched, Dr. Ayer worked on the final report later in the fall 1967.

I came to Thailand to teach at Bangkok Christian College, for a year or so, and now I had spent three years in Thailand and learned a great deal about how it was developing. I was ready to come back to The American University and discuss this process of development. My perspectives were quite unique in that I was not *sent by any one of the three institutions that normally sponsor personnel in developing countries:* **government agencies; businesses; or church institutions.**

I was viewing the developmental process from between the legs of that *three-legged stool.* I do feel it has its hazards, but it is possible! There is probably a fourth leg now, NGOs, i.e., Non-Governmental organizations, but they did not exist in Thailand until I got back in 1971, and we created VOMPOT, (the Volunteer Movement for peoples Organizations in Thailand). I do think developmental thinkers need to reflect on whether it would be wise to venture into countries where **legs** were lacking.

During the three years 1968-1971, I turned down an offered job teaching Personnel management and worked for DETRI, the Development Education & Training Research Institute of A.U. and pursued study of Southeast Asia with Dr. Kenneth P. Landon, Dr. Richard Butwell on Burma, Dr. Lydia NaRanong on Thailand and many other faculty of the School of International Service; and also studied Economic Development with Dr. Warren Hunsberger. Without going into details on courses it should be noted that this was the bulk of the work for the change later concluded moving from a Ph.D. in Public Administration to one in International Relations. While all of this was going on at The American University, Thailand was making major adjustments to build strength to resist Communism, much of it coming from commitments of its own. The data for this study was gathered after I returned to Thailand in 1971, and will constitute Chapter III, Is Thailand the Test Case? But first let us look in detail at the remarkable creation of the Electric Generating Authority in Thailand (EGAT) which has won such respect form Thai people across the entire country.

Thailand Transformed: 1950–2012

Sukhumvit 1972

Chapter II

Yanhee Multi-Purpose River Project – Thailand

The importance of this project is really the administrative mechanism which has been evolving in Thailand. As I related earlier, Yanhee power arrived in Thailand in late December 1964 and it started a major transformation which is still going on. Inexpensive electric power has made, and continues to make important improvement in Thai life. In a Seminar at George Washington University on International Administration I probed deeply into the creation of EGAT, (the Electric Generating Authority of Thailand).

Thailand Struggles for Development

The Yanhee Project was at that time (1970) the largest single IBRD (International Bank for Reconstruction and Development) financed project in Thailand. It was not the first project that IBRD had financed, and it was not financed upon the first request, but only after much careful assessment by the Bank officials over a five year period. The former ambassador to Thailand from the Untied States, Edwin F. Stanton in his Brief Authority, tells of much of the circumstances in the late 1940's and early 1950's as Thailand was struggling to recover from wartime damages and to develop many of its resources with international financial help.[4] The United States extended military assistance to Thailand beginning October 17, 1950[5] and the International Bank granted its first loan to Thailand October 27, 1950.[6] The first IBRD loans amounted to $25,400,000 for railways, irrigation, and port development projects. As these several efforts for economic development were progressing they were having accompanying impact on the local industries and demands were growing for electric power. The independent efforts to satisfy demand in Bangkok and other nearby communities created a patchwork of sources of supply and overlapping of efforts. Somewhere out of the web of customary procedures in Thailand emerged the intention in early 1952 to request another World Bank loan to finance hydroelectric projects.[7]

Royal Irrigation Department Leads in Request for Financing

The initial contacts were made by M.L. Xujati Kambhu to the World Bank (IBRD) in Washington in 1952, with a survey proposal prepared by the Royal Thai Government's Irrigation Department based on the work of several independent engineering consultants. However, the Bank felt that "the project was far from ready for financing."[8] A

---

4   Edwin F. Stanton, *Brief Authority, Excursions of a Common Man in an Uncommon World* (New York: Harpers and Brothers, 1956), p. 233ff and 271ff.
5   *Ibid.* at 256.
6   IBRD, *Eighteenth Annual Report, 1962-1963*, Appendix K, Statement of Loans.
7   James C. Ingram, *Economic Change in Thailand Since 1850*, (Stanford: Stanford University Press, 1955), p. 187. See also for some idea of American Governmental coordination and assistance USOM, *Thai-American Economic and Technical Cooperation* (Bangkok: November 1962), pp. PD 17-18.
8   John A. King, Jr., *Economic Development Projects and Their Appraisal*, (Baltimore: Johns Hopkins Press, 1967), P. 191; See also United States Department of Interior, Bureau of Reclamation, *Yanhee Project, Thailand: Power, Irrigation, Flood Control, and Navigation.* (Denver:USBR, December 1955). p. 34.

second proposal was submitted in early 1953, and it included a much increased electricity production capacity and a much larger construction cost estimate. It is here that the Bank injected its expert judgment and suggested that, "in view of the size and cost of the project in relation to other enterprises in Thailand, there should be an independent study of its economic and engineering merits by outside engineering consultants."[9]

As we see here, the Thai Government officials are working closely with the IBRD engineering consultants and economists in their planning for the financing and construction of the first hydro-electric facility in Southeast Asia to be financed by the World Bank. After the second proposal, one which obviously interested the Bank, Thailand turned to the United States Government and requested the assistance of the highly qualified Bureau of Reclamation in the Department of the Interior. This agency agreed to send a survey team to Thailand in late 1953 to look at proposed sites and decide whether they would agree that Thailand had need for such a project. The initial findings did indicate that the Thai request had sound potentialities, but it was felt a much more detailed survey was needed before such a project could be undertaken and financed. The Thai Government formally requested the assistance of the United States Bureau of Reclamation and a Board of Engineer Consultants was named and sent to Thailand, under United States law as a team of men to train Thai engineers in the work of survey and analysis.[10]

Thus, it seems we are seeing the planning process being carried on by the International Bank officials, the United States Government officials, probably both Embassy and State Department headquarters officials – though records are not accessible, specifically Bureau of Reclamation engineers and Thailand's Royal Irrigation Department officials. In Thailand many offices were drawn into this process, but

---

9   *Ibid.*
10 USDI, ISBR, *Yanhee Project Thailand, op. cit.* Ltr. Of Transmittal; and Interview with A.D. Spottswood, IBRD Engineer Consultant, Feb. 12, 1969.

most prominently were the financial officials, "Boonma in Treasury worked very closely with Xujati on the Yanhee work."[11] together with the experienced irrigation engineers of the Royal Irrigation Department (RID). Social and administrative problems confronting these planners were problems of complexity equaling those which faced the engineers. For Thailand is renowned for its administrative idiosyncrasies Riggs refers to Thailand as a "prismatic society" in its administration,[12] and Ingram merely says, "safeguards are important in view of the nature of administration in Thailand."[13] But it seems the Bank was well advised of these problems, and it was precisely here that the Bank acted to define administrative guidelines to assure that this large loan would be fairly expended to give the nation of Thailand a maximum of development for the investment given to Thailand by the International Bank and its member states.

Bureau of Reclamation Survey

The Bureau of Reclamation survey probed with a thoroughness typical of that experienced American water resources agency, and it completed its comprehensive and valuable study in December 1955, and submitted it to the Royal Thai Government in early 1956. This survey looked at the engineering aspects of the project after detailed probing, test borings and other site measures, to design a structure to meet maximum potentialities and then searched deeply into the economic aspects to determine how Thailand would be able to finance the repayment schedule proposed in a 25-year repayment program usually required by the Bank. The Bureau recommended in its letter of transmittal, due consideration of the Engineer Board's evaluation,

---

11 Spottswood Interview, *op. cit.*
12 Fred W. Riggs, *Administration in Developing Countries*, (Boston: Houghton-Mifflin Co., 1964).
13 Ingram, *op. cit.*, at 187.

The Yanhee Project is considered to be the most desirable and economical development now possible in Thailand for producing electrical power and energy. Cost of the initial phase of development including complete construction of the dam, 140,000 kilowatts of generating capacity, and transmission facilities to Bangkok is estimated to be 454 million bahts and 46.4 million dollars. Future expansion of the power plant and transmission facilities to the ultimate 560,000 kilowatt capacity will require an additional 141 million bahts and 68 million dollars. These figures result in a total equivalent of $257/kw for the developed project. The wholesale cost of energy at primary distribution busses required to repay the project in 25 years with interest at 5 per cent is estimated to be 0.262 bahts/kwh. By comparison, a modern fuel-electric power system designed to serve only the heavy population center at Bangkok for a similar period (with 340,000 kw capacity) would require a wholesale rate of 0.329 bahts/kwh. Furthermore, once the initial costs have been repaid, the cost of producing Yanhee power would be reduced to less than one-fourth of the initial rate, while the fuel-electric rate could be dropped only 15 per cent.

It is the Board's recommendation that the features and basic designs, as described in this report, be the basis for the development of the Yanhee Project, both initially and ultimately. With such a development of the Yanhee Project, the Board believes that the national interests of Thailand will best be served in alleviating the present power deficiency, as well as providing a means for developing and expanding the future economy of the country.[14]

With the USBR Yanhee Report, which had been carefully prepared by American engineers working side by side with Thai engineers in an important training process, the Royal Irrigation Department of Thailand

---

14 *Yanhee Project, Thailand*, Letter of/Transmittal, *op. cit.*

approached the Bank a third time for a loan. The Bank was now ready to begin its own survey work. In 1956 the IBRD sent its survey team to Thailand to "appraise the situation and report back prior to any agreement to finance." [15] Their report indicated that this looked like a very good project and that Bangkok was in need of this kind of a power source.

International Bank Guidance and Financing

In late 1956 and during most of the year 1957, the Bank officers worked to prepare an agreement with appropriate safeguards and requirements to give administrative guidelines for this project's financing. Specifically, the loan was to be one initially for $66,000,000 with a four-year grace period and then repayment over a 21-year period. Administratively, the Bank established six requirements for Thailand, before the loan could be authorized.[16]

1- Thailand must agree to establish a Yanhee Electricity Authority to manage the power generation, distribution and sale.
2- Construction of the Yanhee facility must be handled by the Royal Irrigation Department, who in turn would handle subcontracting.
3- The distribution system must be improved throughout the area and it must be done by major construction efforts, as specified by IBRD.
4- The Bangkok Municipal Power System must be turned over to the Yanhee Electricity Authority. ("It was a corrupt, graft-ridden outfit.")
5- The IBRD specified that the Board of Directors of the YEA could not be ranking government officials, as is a pattern elsewhere in Thai business.

---

15 Spottswood Interview, *op. cit.*
16 *Ibid.*

6- The IBRD also sets very strict controls on funds for any loans they make, but this was especially true on this first large loan to Thailand. Once a loan is made, the borrower can not get his hands on any money:

    i-The borrowing government must specify to IBRD what they will need to buy, by category of item;

    ii-IBRD insists that large orders must then go to international competitive bidding;

    iii – Payments then can be made on billing direct to the IBRD, or they can be made to the government revolving fund which shows debits for expenses recorded in certified form.

    iv – Any money left over must be cancelled at the end of construction.

With these details worked out and Thailand in agreement, the loan was negotiated September 12, 1957 for $66,000,000 at 5-3/4% interest, repayment to begin after four-years of grace for construction. It is important to also note that the Bank kept an official in Bangkok for many years to monitor the handling of these loans, but that Thai management is so successful that he is no longer felt necessary for this purpose. Initially, Thailand was required to secure Bank approval of all extensions of more than 30 MW over the initial 140 MW, but after the careful handling of the first two requests, each for 70 MW, this requirement was removed and Thailand has managed that decision process well.[17] Mr. A.D. Spottswood, the IBRD Engineer Consultant for this particular Yanhee Project spoke particularly warmly of the two successive Directors of the Yanhee Electricity Authority, saying that these two men, M.L.Xujati Kambhu and Kasem Chakrivati, have been forthright with good common-sense, and they have had the confidence of the top officials. Both men have worked to keep political influence

---

17   *Ibid.*

out of these matters and have maintained a high standard of integrity. Kasem in particular has done well, not having the extra element of being a member of the royal family as was M.L.Xujati Kambhu.[18] Kasem has recruited exceptionally fine and honest young people to manage the Yanhee Electricity Authority, and with their help he has been able to plan carefully, justify fully and defend his actions so that he has impressed governmental officers as a most able administrator.

Measures of the Success of the IBRD Guidance

So successful has been this quiet, independent guidance and administrative restraint used by the IBRD, that Thailand as a borrower is now known (in 1970), to come to the Bank and ask assistance to finance a project, whereafter Thailand purchases more than half of the issue themselves. Yet the Thai officials feel that "We need you (IBRD)!" They actually feel that they need us for our discipline in financing. They can then say, "Well, we have to do it this way, because of the Bank's demands." In essence, the Bank provides a necessary lever for disciplined administration in a country still beset by social and administrative traditions which cause problems for efficient development activity.

Thus, we have seen how the IBRD moved to aid Thailand in its postwar development beginning October 27, 1950 and how the administrative guidance of the Bank helped reshape the proposal of the Royal Irrigation Department for a hydropower facility in 1952, until it had a design in hand which would maximize a water resources potential. Therewith, Thailand gained for its economic development the best resource that could be harnessed to give electric power in west central Thailand. This has only been the beginning of the power development story in Thailand, because today, Yanhee Electricity Authority, in its new form as EGAT (Electric Generating Authority

---

18   *Ibid.*

of Thailand) manages many supplies of power to satisfy a demand far exceeding any expectations in 1957 when the loan was granted. Bangkok currently uses at its peak period daily, more than 600 MW of power and Yanhee supplies at those peak periods 280 MW. The remainder is managed by the same well-run EGAT, but produced by a variety of alternative methods, from steam turbines (240 MW), gas turbines (60 MW), to diesel generators (20 MW). And, even that is barely satisfying the needs in 1970, so that EGAT has 600 MW of power plants under construction: the final 140 MW for Yanhee Dam, 400 MW in thermal generation, and 60 MW in gas turbines. Recent years have seen other hydropower projects in Thailand and in Laos from which power is transmitted across the Mekong River into Thailand to meet its industrial growth and urban demands.

Yanhee has many successes for Thailand. It not only brought more power, but it has helped to regularize administration of this vital resource and to bestow a pride of accomplishment on its builders, whether engineers, administrators, or economists. It was a great task, well accomplished and with many of the implications for future changes needed in Thai administration for even greater development.[19]

The process of planning for Yanhee did not go beyond these initial administrative, cultural, and engineering hurdles, that is, to processes of social and educational planning. The planning process did not include work for any inter-related social and educational development. Yanhee's planners contented themselves with building a great hydro-electric production facility and an administrative mechanism which could stand as an example of what can be done to promote development without corrupt practices and to do it as expeditiously as was humanly possible. Inherent in all of the construction and administrative work done by

---

19 Albert O. Hirschman, *Developoment Projects Observed* (Washington: Brookings Institution, 1967) Chatper One, "The Principle of the Hiding Hand," and at 167; and James Morris, *The Road to Huddersfield, A Journey to Five Continents*. (New York: Pantheon Books, 1963). *P. 214.*

American consultants and IBRD advisors was training- for Thais. The chief engineer for construction has commented that, "…these Thai engineers progressed rapidly and when the project was finished they were able to be employed on the construction of a refinery in south-central Thailand at Sriracha."[20] Thus, even without formally planning to educate with projects of this nature – in countries where the rudiments of training have been given its people, as Thailand has done – we see education in capital project construction contributing to raise the quality of manpower resources by the very process of working side by side with highly skilled technicians.

Why Is Thailand the Test Case?

The history in this next chapter was researched in 1963, before I went to Thailand because I had developed an interest in Thailand through Church work and an international law case I had worked on at Covington & Burling on Khao Preah Vihear (temple ruins) for Dean Acheson and his colleagues. And then in 1973-74 I contracted with USOM-Thailand to computerize their Thai training records and built the accurate record of 25 years of education and training work conducted for Thais by that Operations Mission, 1950-1975. When you look at Tables 2, 3, and 4 you begin to see the impact education has had on Thailand and its middle class, and how those twenty-five years has made it possible to look for a growth of constitutionalism and democracy in this corner of Southeast Asia.[21]

---

20 Interview and public comments of Mr. Carl Lovitt, Chief Engineer for Yanhee and currently, Vice President, Sverdrup & Parcel, Inc. at the International Conference, University of Pittsburgh, October 23, 1968; *Cf*., Morris, *op. cit.* at 131.
21 Chapter III, "Is Thailand the Test Case?" was prepared for an Association for Asian Studies Conference held at George Washington University, October 2003.

Chapter III

Is Thailand the Test Case?

Dr. Culver S. Ladd   October 2003

With the end of the Second World War in August 1945, Asia was in much turmoil. Secretary of State Dean Acheson speaking January 12, 1950 at the national Press Club in Washington, D.C. and citing General Douglas MacArthur on a defensive perimeter, drew a line through the Aleutians to Japan and then on to the Ryukyus to the Philippines. Importantly his speech was titled, "Crisis in China – An Examination of United States Policy," and included these paragraphs:

> So far as the military security of other areas in the Pacific is concerned, it must be clear that no person can guarantee these areas against military attack...
>
> Should such an attack occur...the initial reliance must be on the people attacked to resist it and then upon the commitments of the entire civilized world under the Charter of the United nations, which so far has not proved a weak reed to lean on by people who are determined to protect their independence against outside aggression.

On June 25, 1950, North Korean forces equipped with Soviet-made weapons invaded South Korea. The Soviet United Nations representative Yakov A. Malik had been boycotting the Security Council and on June 25, the Council ordered an immediate cease-fire and the withdrawal of all North Korean forces. On June 27, the U.N. Security Council called upon members to "furnish such assistance as may be necessary to the Republic of Korea to repel the armed attack and to restore international peace and security in the area."[22]

General Douglas MacArthur was designated U.N. Commander on July 8, 1950, and the Soviet representative began blocking all further actions after his return on August 1, 1950.

Thailand's Emergence on the World Scene in Asia

Importantly for this study on Thailand, is the history that immediately upon receiving the United Nations call for assistance, Thailand wired back that Thailand would send volunteers. Field Marshal Pibul Songkhram crystallized a new Thai principle of Defense against Communism. The United States had an ally, and it has waxed and waned since then as the years passed. But as long as the United States was militarily involved in Asia, Thailand has stood with them.

Defense Against Communism

A series of articles appeared in the Virginia Quarterly Review in 1950 and 1951, dealing with American policy toward South-East Asia. Those articles were very important at that time in shaping American attitudes toward that area, and its strategic importance. By mid-1950, the Korean War was going toward a Communist victory. The suggestion that, "Southeast Asia dominates several of the principal sea and air routes in the world…if this region were lost, no airfields at all would be available between India and Australia. One of the most important

---

22 Acheson, Dean, Present At The Creation, New York: Norton, 1969. p. 357.

ocean routes of the world runs through the Straits of Malacca...trade of every nation...eventually finds itself in the South China Sea east of Singapore."[23] Put the reader in a frame of mind to read on. And as he did so, he began to understand the vital economic interdependence that Southeast Asia had in the world: an important economic factor.

"...is that Malaya is the principal dollar earner in the whole British Empire. Its sales of tin and rubber to the United States provides more dollars than the exports of Britain herself. One aim of the present Communist uprising in Malaya has been to injure Britain's economic recovery by wrecking the tin and rubber industries..."[24]

Early in 1951, another important article appeared in this review, suggesting, "with the Communist conquest of China, Southeast Asia became a region of crucial importance in world politics...Standards of living throughout the region are low and everywhere, with the exception of Thailand, there is active unrest."[25] Author Vandenbosch asked, "In view of these basic facts, what hope is there that the region will not go Communist?" He then posed a solution:

> "In many respects Thailand presents a test case. Conditions here are more favorable than in any of the neighboring countries. It has no background of political colonialism it is still peaceful, and its general economic conditions, judged by Oriental standards, are not bad. Living conditions must be improved but they are not yet acute. It would seem that if the will to resist Communism is not present among the Siamese, or if their will to resist cannot be aided effectively by outside help, there is nothing that can be done to prevent the ascendancy of Communism in any of the countries of the region."

23　Morris, Richard B., Encyclopedia of American History, New York: Harper & Row, 1976. p. 477.
24　Mills, Lennox A., "The Cold War in Southeast Asia," Va.Q.Rev., Vol. 26, No. 3, Summer 1950, p.366.
25　Ibid.

But to achieve this, he suggested the burden would be great and of long duration. "The pleasant idea we have entertained so far that a little technical aid will do the trick is wholly erroneous. Either we go in a very large scale or withdraw altogether."[26]

By the time this second article appeared, the United States had negotiated three important treaties with Thailand. June 1950, saw a Fulbright Education Treaty; September 1950 saw first, an Economic and Technical Assistance Treaty, and then a Military Assistance Treaty. The United States was moving very fast to deter Communism on the southern edge of China.[27]

The creation of the Southeast Asia Treaty Organization in 1954 had quite an obvious influence on aid giving by the United States. The American military expenditures do not show as dramatic a change, but they do reveal the growing concern of the Thai with their own security, in terms of their comparable budget expenditures for defense. Table 1 shows how giving and commitment changes from 1951 for two decades:

---

26 Vandenbosch, Amry, "Thailand, The Test Case," Va.Q.Rev., Vol. 27, No. 1, Winter 1951, p.27.
27 Ibid.,p. 37.; CF., Alastair Buchan, "The Indochina War and World Politics," Foreign Affairs, Vol. 53, p. 639, regarding Japanese security (1975).

Table 1
U.S. Military & Economic Aid Compared to RTG Defense Commitments
($ Millions)

Year	Regular Military Assistance	U.S. Summary of Economic Aid (Operating, Investment, Construction, Overhead and Excess Property)	RTG Defense Budget Actual Expenditures	U.S. Mil. as % RTG Def. Budget.
1951	4.5	1.7	12.3	37
1961	49.0	...	69.2	70
1971	61.6	68.2	269.3	23

Source: J. Alexander Caldwell, American Economic Aid to Thailand, Lexington, Mass.: Lexington Books, 1974. p. 29.

Thailand Transformed: 1950-2012

This willingness to spend increasingly on defense, shows that the Thais are beginning to feel they can continue their independence, politically, and probably maintain a measure of control over the "threat" which Communist China was posing, with increasing imminence.[28] China has historically been Thailand's most powerful neighbor, and the specter of a strong, united China has long haunted the Thai. It was the Mongols who drove the Thais southout of Yunnan.

This entire twenty year period of intense American involvement saw very slight inflation, and the steadily improving ability to build defense capabilities as well as maintaining its other commitments domestically show that the Thai have learned vital military lessons well.

The United States military has taught Thailand that high level military technology has direct correlation for industrial planning. Thus, the military planner is providing basic strength for industrial development in areas as wide-ranging as automotives and food-processing, and functioning in coordination with the Ministry of Industries. Thailand in the late 1970s was strongly able to manage its governmental policies. The test of its readiness and abilities to stand against the "red tide" was then upon Thailand. The Kingdom of Laos converted to a democratic people's republic and the King was forced to abdicate in December 1975. Whether the building process had been a successful one since 1950 was then tested. It has now stood for an additional thirty years since the end of the Battle in Vietnam.[29]

Creating an Environment for Diversification

The post World War II conditions of the Thailand monetary system was substantial disarray. Its funds in banks in Japan, England, and the United States were frozen, and it had only about 33 million in gold in

---

28 Compare, Arthur Huck, "China and the Chinese Threat System," International Affairs, Vol. 49, No. 4, (1973). P. 617.
29 Swain, Jon, "Final Piece in the Asian Jig-Saw," The Sunday Times, London: December 7, 1975. p. 9

Bangkok for a reserve behind its currency. Thailand had traditionally not financed itself by borrowing, but had exported to earn a surplus in balance of payments. Its financial training was conducted by Great Britain during the nineteenth century, and it learned well the lessons of how to manage its sterling accounts.[30]

The problem which confronted Thailand in the postwar period was, how to put the financial system into order without causing inflation and yet to promote development. In the broad sense, the need of an effective monetary system is the development of a variety of financial institutions across the country to assist in the reallocation of resources to more efficient uses. The fundamental need was to motivate individuals to hold assets in financial rather than in real form, that is, to make savings more attractive than gold. The Bank of Thailand established a twelve-months fixed deposit policy for commercial and savings institutions, earning 6.5% to 11% or higher at various periods of the past decade of the 1960s; while dropping the interest rate on regular savings accounts to only 2.75% per annum. Suffice it to say, that this has reached deeply into the practices of rural areas, and helped farm people earn interest on their savings.

At the same time, Thailand was holding to a most controversial policy on rice marketing. It is referred to as the "rice premium" policy, and it has worked to maintain domestic price stability on the principal food item in the Thai diet. The friendly greeting in Western countries is often, "How are you?", but in the Thai society, as in the Chinese society, it is usually, "Have you eaten?" The item eaten, is usually rice, and at all meals. While maintaining domestic price on rice, Thailand was being aided in diversifying its agricultural products. Among the first Thais brought to the United States for training under the economic aid programs were farmers of pineapples to improve their skills.

---

30 Ingram, James, <u>Economic Change in Thailand, 1850-1870</u>, Stanford: Stanford University Press, 1971.

It is important to note here the quality of training that Thais were being given under the economic aid programs: a research soils laboratory, Bangkhen Experiment Station, Soils Fertility & Management practices, Northeast Agricultural Development, rice improvement, Protein food Development, Fishery Development, Potable Water, are among several hundred projects which by 1971 comprised more than the actual U.S. military Assistance (see Table 1).

This education and training process is the critical element assisting a nation to modernize and in essence "develop." In the case of Thailand this process was initiated through a dozen or more university contracts. See Table 2, on the next page.

TABLE 2

Contract Purpose	Contracting University/College
Improvement of Kasetsart University	OREGON STATE COLLEGE/UNIVERSITY OF HAWAII
Agricultural Research	University of Kentucky
Family Planning	University of North Carolina
Chiang Mai Medical School	University of Illinois
SEATO Skilled Labor(Regional)	University of Hawaii
Improve Technical Education	Wayne State University
IBRD Vocational Education	Oklahoma State/ California State Poly Universities
ASIAN Institute of Technology	Colorado State University
Teacher Training	Indiana University
Improve Chulalongkorn University (Engineering Department)	University of Texas
Establish Facilities to Improve English Language Training	University of Michigan
Education Research & Planning	Michigan State University
Institute of Public Administration	Indiana University

Source: USOM-Thailand, Compiled May 23, 1974, personal files of Dr. Ladd.

Having said this, let us look at a table showing how many Thais were trained from 1950 to October 31, 1975.

TABLE 3

Participant Training Inventory Totals As of October 31, 1975					
PARTICIPANTS TRAINED					
Participants Returned from Training	9,867	Male	8,279	Female	1,588
Total Participants	9,867	Male	8,279	Female	1,588
PARTICIPANT PROGRAMS COMPLETED	Participants		PROGRAMS		
Participants trained only one time	8,467		8,467		
Participants trained two times	1,088		2,176		
Participants trained three times	239		717		
Participants trained four times	57		228		
Participants trained five times	11		55		
Participants trained over five times	5		31		
TOTAL Participants	9,867		11,674		
CURRENT STATUS OF RETURNED PARTICIPANTS					
Royal Thai Government Employees	8,311		Resigned		514
Private Enterprise & Farm Employees	308		Abroad		20
Other (Int'l & U.S. Gov't)	65		Deceased		238
Retired	381		TOTAL	Reported:	9,837
Source: USOM-Thailand, Dr. Ladd file					

Thailand Transformed: 1950-2012

TABLE 4

Trained Participants by Field of Training and Qualifications Received as of October 1975.

LEVEL OF QUALIFIC- ATION	DIRECT MILITARY SUPPORT	AGRICUL- TURE NATURAL RESOURCE	INDUSTRY MINING	TRANS- PORTA- TION	LABOR	HEALTH SANITA- TION	EDUCA- TION	PUBLIC SAFETY PUBLIC ADMIN.	COMMUN- ITY DEV- ELOP- MENT	PVT. ENTER- PRISE	GENERAL TOTALS: BY DEGREE TRAINING
PHD/MD	1	33				9	31	11	2	7	93
MA/MS		372	53	5	1	97	674	128	143	106	1580
BA/BS		14	1	1		7	25	1	16	1	66
OJT/OBS	9	1689	219	235	44	1199	810	1454	886	281	6826
TOTALS:	10	2108	273	241	45	1312	1540	1594	1047	395	8565

SOURCE: USOM-Thailand, Compiled May 23, 1974, Personal Files of Dr. Ladd

The important element of this training to be noted now in retrospective is that every Changwad in Thailand had participants trained. In many cases that training consisted of Third Country Observation tours by farmers, to orient them about new farming practices. Twenty-five farmers were brought to the United States for a tour of three months and placed in farm fields in New Jersey with garden crops, and in Iowa especially to observe corn production.

That quality of practical exposure now returning to farm fields in Thailand has helped to move local level Thais to new visions of what could be accomplished in their own farm work. And, it has meant that the entire country has been influenced to think of better possibilities in their personal lives and communities.

Participant Training Inventories

How do the Thais feel about the training they have received. In a Participant Training Program Survey Evaluation completed after ten years of the program, 1951-1960, "Ninety-two per cent of the participants interviewed say that they have *used something* in their current jobs. Sixty-two per cent say they have used quite-a-bit or almost everything."

"Ninety-four per cent of the participants say that they have conveyed something acquired in training to others." and, "Over sixty per cent mention two or more ways in which their training has been passed along, and conveyance in a 'formal' situation best characterizes the procedure followed (Comprises 75% of the mentions).[31]

Interestingly, "Almost all (over 99%) of the participants interviewed were given employment on their return and have never been unemployed… (a) job shift resulted in a "better" job in three out of every four cases. Ninety-seven per cent of the participants were working for the Thai Government at the time of the interview, and, in general, participants

---

31 Ayer, Frederic L., Participant Training Program, Thailand 1951-1960, An Evaluation Survey, Vol. 1, Bangkok: Business Research Ltd., 1963. p. 69.

were working at the time of the interview in the same "kind of work" they were doing at the time of selection.[32]

Thailand's Rapid Growth Linked to Prudent Policies

The International Monetary Fund in its Survey of December 11, 1995, says,

> By all measures, Thailand's growth over the past three decades has been impressive. Averaging 7.25 percent annual growth over this period. Thailand saw its per capita income increase fivefold. (added). Resilient and pragmatic, the Thai economy has relied on a vigorous private sector and a firm and enduring commitment to macroeconomic stability to transform itself from a heavy dependence on a narrow agricultural base to one that now includes significant manufacturing and service sectors. A solid policy foundation positioned the country in the late 1980s to take advantage of a major shift in production within the East Asian region. The consequent economic boom firmly established Thailand's position in the second wave of East Asian "tigers." * * *

"The rapid growth that Thailand has enjoyed over the past several decades has not been without environmental and social costs, particularly in Bangkok, which has been the focal point for development. Further growth will necessitate a greater geographic dispersion for development and heavier investment in infrastructure throughout the country."

And, in conclusion the IMF Survey, adds,

> Thailand's exceptionally rapid and sustained development reflects its long-standing commitment to prudent financial management and steadily, and pragmatically, pursued structural reform… Finally, Thailand is cognizant that rising wage costs will necessitate a shift over time to a larger technological component in production. The government has moved, decisively and

---

32   Ibid.

innovatively, to address the country's related education and training needs. Thailand's open trading regime and its increased exposure to international competition should also assist in this continuing process of economic transformation."[33]

No real indication of the crisis which was to descend upon Thailand eighteen months later. But, the IMF has stood ready to help when a crisis occurred. The fund's performance in Asia has highlighted its three essential roles: First, the IMF offers macroeconomic policy advice which any good politician can use to sell to voters as their own, Second, the IMF acts as a global lender of last resort during a liquidity crunch, much like a national central bank plays in a domestic crisis. And, third, the IMF promotes microeconomic reforms that might otherwise be politically unacceptable.[34]

<u>Thailand, The Crisis Leader.</u> The July 1997 devaluation of the Thai baht (from $1=20Baht; to the current 2003 $1=42Baht) started a global financial contagion that triggered sudden collapses across Asian currencies. All of which led to a rash of bankruptcies among corporations and financial institutions. This in turn contributed to a general slide in world commodity prices.

In reality the Asian crisis stemmed from private-sector mismanagement. As we look at Bangkok's transformation from a sleepy SEA capital in the 1950-1970 era, now in the 1990s a large metropolis of 6 million, we see the hand of Linne Tholin, retired Chief City Engineer of Chicago, who taught the Thai how to build buildings. And buildings they have built, even as big as 66 floors.

---

[33] <u>IMF Survey,</u> Washington, D.C.: International Monetary Fund, Vol. 24, No. 23. December 11, 1995. Pp. 389-392.
[34] Hale, David D., "The IMF, Now More than Ever," <u>Foreign Affairs,</u> Vol. 77, No. 6, December 1998, p. 7-13.

Thailand Transformed: 1950–2012

But, an NPL is a non-performing loan, and when a bank has many NPLs and the building owners do not have any ideas about occupancy of their fine new building, banks crash! This has been the major cause of the crisis in Thailand and it still has not been completely resolved.

"The surplus global liquidity and low cost borrowing encouraged reckless allocation of capital, including speculative real estate ventures (Thailand), ill-conceived industrial projects (South Korea) and crony capitalist networks that based investment decisions on political relationships rather than purely commercial criteria(Indonesia and Malaysia)…Thailand (has) maintained global market access, begun recapitalizing their econom(y), and rolled over a large volume of their existing bank loans. Thailand has attracted over $8 billion in foreign capital since March (1998) for bank equity recapitalization buyouts of bankrupt companies, and sales of defaulted finance company loans.[35]

Regretably Thai taxpayers are picking up a share of these adjustment costs.

Problems of Political and Administrative Development

We all realize that economic change is a potent stimulant to a general social change. And the United States has been focally working at this in Thailand since 1950. Thai leadership has long realized a need to modernize. King Mongkut in the 19th century was one of the wisest leaders in Southeast Asia. He brought in foreign advisors and that practice was carried on by his son King Chulalongkorn. Thailand kept its independence because it was looking for modern ways to change. Only too often in the 20th century, military coups have taken place and development and reform are only minor factors in the thinking of

---

35 Ibid., p. 9-10.

military leaders. Fear of change and reform dominate the traditional elites, and the lack of experience tend to conspire to limit the number of political leaders available for the new tasks, often difficult and complex ones of managing a modern government.[36]

And that was our focus in the training programs. Could we prepare the administrative staffs and a broad ranging segment of Thai society to tolerate change?[37]

Yet the Thai case is unique because the "tolerance of controversy" has been part of Thai society since the Royal Proclamation of October 8, 1878 which established toleration of all religious faiths pursuant to the martyrdom of two men converts to Christianity in Chiang Mai by the priesthood. This has been incorporated in all constitutions of Thailand since 1932, and it is reaffirmed in the current one.

This process of change in cognitive styles, from intolerance toward tolerance has been examined in cross-cultural evaluations over many years in graduate students of less developed countries leaving the United States for their home country. Suffice it to say here, that there is a wide gap in thinking from traditional to modern thought,

> "…Everyone of us, educated people, with degrees from abroad come back to this country and normally enter the bureaucracy. As soon as we enter the bureaucracy we are submerged by it. No more the dissenting voice. No more the independent thinking. We're submerged in this whole system…"[38]

---

36 CF., Landon, Kenenth P., Southeast Asia: Crossroads of Religions, Chicago: University of Chicago Press, 1949, p. 169; Promsiri, Trirat, Thailand's Transition, Bangkok: Prae Pittaya LP, February 1965, p. 23; and Wilson, David A., The United States and the Future of Thailand, New York: Praeger, 1970. P. 141 et seq.
37 Wells, Kenneth E., The History of Protestant Work in Thailand, Bangkok: Christian Press, 1960. Pp. 59-62.
38 Glenn, Edmund S., Robert H. Johnson, Paul R. Kimmel, and Bryant Wedge, "A Cognitive Interaction Model to Analyze Cultural Conflict in International Relations," The Journal of Conflict Resolution, Vol. XIV, No. 1, March 1970. P. 42 and p. 85.

Since this condition is a true one, how do you move members of a society to simply act in new ways? The answer is that you simply have to restructure whole segments of the society to buttress these individuals, and help them to act out their newly learned roles! Does that mean you must have a communist leadership to accomplish those changes? The American case shows that society, evolving into a free-enterprise, independent nation, without communism. The Thai case shows a similar transition without communism.

Both the American and the Thai cases reveal the institution of constitutional government, with civilianized leadership, and an active legislative body, to manage the country during crucial periods of external threat to domestic security. Freedom of speech, assembly, petition, and freedom of religious practice are all constitutionally guaranteed in these two cases. To arrive at this desired point of tolerance, the society had to sustain conditioning: in the Thailand case, conditioning by students' demonstrations; worker strikes; urban squatter petitions; and the removal by citizens' revolution of leadership with a "low threshold" of tolerance, namely the military leaders who were forced out of the country, or 'civilianized' in the country. This process actually continued until 1997. Then Thailand led the world into a crisis no military leader was capable of solving, and civilians have now succeeded civilians without coup since then.

The Thailand case has shown that during the economic development of Thailand, many new channels for socialization became a part of the society, as industry entered to employ new techniques and teach Thai new ways of behaving in these industrial contexts. The whole process of American assistance giving, included agencies of government acting as "schools" in a new cultural invasion into Thailand. This process permeated the educational system; the bureaucracy at many points, but most effectively by drawing functions concerned with development projects together into a Ministry of National Development; the local changwad administrative systems, by developing "counter-insurgency" mechanism in local areas and teaching a process of information flow both up and down the hierarchy; movie theaters, and American student groups all setting a style and mode of behavior which has made new social customs acceptable and broadened tolerance among even the most conservative Thai.[39]

Creating Community

The outcome of all these endeavors was the Student Revolution of 1973 and the well-guided efforts to "teach democracy" which is taking able college graduates and helping them start a career in local areas of Thailand to bring the country-side into a participant role in Thailand political life.[40]

At the same time, labor organizations in Thailand, started in 1968 and thwarted in the Coup of 1971, saw a renewal after the Student Revolution, and they have grown and been frustrated during the coups since then. But, out of all this turmoil has come an establishment of Non-Governmental Organizations in 2000 that have won respect for poor people and for refugees living in Thailand.

> "If one reviews the evolution of the concept of community, it seems evident that it is central to much political thought. Only radically individualist and skeptical thinkers have failed to assign to community the kind of position which the space-time continuum occupies in physics – it is the thing <u>within</u> which political events

---

39 Cf., Almond, Gabriel A. and Sidney Verba, <u>The Civic Culture: Political Attitudes and Democracy in Five Nations,</u> Princeton: Princeton University Press, 1963. P. 501; Compare, Fred Warren Riggs, <u>Administration in Developing Countries. The Theory of Prismatic Society,</u> Boston: Houghton-Mifflin Company, 1964. 477 Pages, and Culver S. Ladd, "The Evolution of Constitutional Forms of Government, with Special Reference to Asian Countries Considered in the Light of the Experience of Third World Countries Generally," Ph.D. Thesis, Ann Arbor, MI: University Microfilms, 1984.

40 Zimmerman, Robert F., "Student 'Revolution' in Thailand: The End of the Thai Bureaucratic Polity?" <u>Asian Survey,</u> Vol. XIV, No. 6, June 1974. Pp. 509-529.

> occur – and the kind of position which life occupies in biology – it is the thing <u>upon</u> which all the political goings-on depend. That is why, like space and life, it has often been referred to as a "mystery" springing directly from some basic ineluctable disposition of human beings. The <u>dzoon politikon</u> as which Aristotle saw man cannot be thought of outside its political community; anyone trying to live such a separate life would be either a God or a beast." -Carl J. Friedrich.[41]

It is this quality of "mysterious" oneness, which makes the nation function; and it is this oneness, which is sought in "constitutional governments," and in the efforts of "communist" leaders who are striving to build national entities. The process can be seen as evolutionary or revolutionary: That is, given "controversy" it should be possible as in the Thailand case to "evolve" toward a functioning constitutional state system; this must be seen in contra-distinction to the "violent revolution" of all sectors of society, in the Chinese and Russian models, as now being applied in Indo-China. It should be possible to see "balanced growth," not only politically, but also economically and societally, toward a healthy and viable free constitutional system, in other areas of the developing world.

This Mysterious Oneness

The "mysterious" oneness, or "mysterious" sympathy, which is the founding quality which makes the community a place where law is respected and where the expression of civil liberties is fully possible, must not be extinguished; because the oneness of the leaders must not only allow it – but value it – in that it contributes to the essential "controversy," which is the life of the community. Thus, the whole possibility of success in constitutional government is wrapped up in the concern of the community in its expression of justice for the members

---

41   Friedrich, Carl J., (ed.), <u>Community</u>, NOMOS II, New York: Liberal Arts Press, 1959. p. 22 ff.

of the community. In the theological sense, Reinhold Niebuhr has put it this way,

"(In an industrial civilization and in an age of nuclear terror, the renewal of the church must certainly include full awareness of the fact that we are all involved in the virtues and the vices, the guilt and the promise of our generation. In a sense it is true that we cannot be saved unless we are all saved."[42]

It is that concern, which enlivens the community, nation, and international community, and gives it the possibility of being. Without it, communism poses a clear alternative by managing all of life, and super-imposing a "new order" with new leaders. In this new century, it is Muslim terrorism which poses a much less formal threat; at this point it is without the formal philosophical basis which Marx and Mao had bestowed on Communism of the last century.

All Things Considered – Thailand's New Order

The latest Constitution drafted in 1997, is Thailand's 16th such document since 1932, coming after 17 coups, and 53 governments. It was adopted just as the economy collapsed. The baht lost half its value, half of the country's loans turned sour and output plummeted. Two successful governments have now operated under this Constitution. It is a 171-page document with 336 articles reflecting a strong mistrust of those who hold authority and a clear determination to spread power thinly across the changewads and monitor the exercise of authority closely. For example, section 30: "Unjust discrimination against a person on the grounds of difference in origin, race, language, sex, age, physical or health condition, personal status, economic or social standing, religious belief, education or constitutionally political view shall not be permitted." The Constitution focused on the parliament, the electoral

---

42 Niebuhr, Reinhold, "The Conditions of Our Survival," <u>Virginia Quarterly Review,</u> Vol. 26, No. 4, Autuum 1950. Pp. 481-491.

system, the courts, the cabinet, the bureaucracy, local administration – in short, almost everything the government does and is involved in in stimulating economic growth and society development.

People Power

"Teach democracy" efforts of the 1960s and 1970s, is institutionalized in the Constitution with its aim to "decentralize powers to localities," and "develop a large-sized local government." The share of government revenues in local hands is being steadily increased, from around 10% to 20% in 2001 and targeted for 35% by 2006.

"As the term of each of Thailand's 7,951 appointed local councils expires, elections are being held to replace them." At the same time the government is drawing up plans to decentralize the police, health care and education, aiming eventually to place these services under local control.[43]

The Constitution is an extraordinary document, and it encourages citizens to take an active role in their governance, monitoring and challenging the bureaucracy. It establishes rights to "get access to public information," "to participate in the decision-making process of state officials," "to present a petition," "to sue state agencies," and even to "receive explanation and reasons from a state agency before permission is given for any project." Populist actions like: initiative and recall are permitted with 50,000 signatures in the nation of 60 million.

The formerly appointed Senate, or Upper House of Parliament, now has got to go through the election process, without the backing of a political party. That change has opened the door to NGO activists, human-rights lawyers, even journalists are being elected to influence the process even with their expertise in rallying public sentiments.[44]

---

43   The Economist, A New Order, A Survey of Thailand," March 2, 2002. P. 5.
44   Ibid.

How Do You Clean Up Corruption

As is the case in many less developed countries, governments lack effective tax methods and are unable to pay their employees an adequate wage for their services to the public. A common practice is to award an office to a relative or politically connected person which is in essence a "sinecure" or position where bribes are taken for services. Usually this occurs with police, immigration officers, and other administrative function like awarding new house numbers, or in the Thai case, "auspicious" house numbers. Of course, I had repeated instances where bribes were sought, but I was always able to resist. An interesting case occurred on the World Bank-financed water system for Bangkok. I had done a steel study in 1973 and had inquired of the Boston engineering firm designing the system, how much steel was being planned for the water system. Not much, I was told, the pipes were to be "concrete," but the valves were Steel. He discussed how they were planning it. A year or so later, I was contacted to help a contracting firm determine how many valves of each type were needed, because the Thai administrator of the contracting process could not tell them for their bidding. I met with the Thai official and he was unable to tell me either. And so, with the aid of the Engineer's Handbook I specified exactly how many valves of each type would be required and the firm entered accurate bids. Thailand has serious problems with this type of corruption.

The Constitution establishes two controversial new agencies to clean up political life: The Election Commission and the National Counter-Corruption Commission (NCCC). The government has no control of the work of these two agencies, and members are selected to minimize political influence. The Election Commission actually invalidated 78 out of 200 results in the 2000 election. One constituency actually had re-runs five times. Every creative effort is being employed by the Bangkok mandarins to throttle these agencies, with budget controls and political appointments having some limited effects. The broad base of Thais now in 2003 with their enlarged middle class, are demanding respect for the documents.

The NCCC issued a ruling on Thaksin Shinawatra, Thailand's current Prime Minister, had not accurately disclosed his assets, and in only a few days thereafter, he was elected Prime Minister. That put the burden on the Constitutional Court to rule on the NCCC charges. The Court by a split vote overturned the NCCC ruling and allowed him to retain his office.

The fact that the Constitution even exists is remarkable, and it only exists because the financial collapse occurred at that same time. Elites were too consumed with financial problems to work to block a popular Constitution. A time-honored practice of party switching has been ended, where the new constitution automatically bars a switcher from competing in subsequent by-elections. And MPs who accept ministerial roles must resign from parliament. Mr. Thaksin has rallied with his Thai Rak Thai Party to win 248 seats, just three shy of an overall majority. Then Seritham party with 14 members folded into TRT and he had a solid majority. This elimination of switching has ushered in a whole new era in politics in Thailand. Thaksin is using his political muscle and accomplishing much for local level constituents, and for the country as a whole.

Adjusting the Economy After the Crash

To get some idea of the measures being employed by Thailand to solve its financial crisis, let us take note of actions by the Thai Assets Management Corporation, created with the advice of the IMF to solve the 1997 Financial Crisis. BangkokPost.com reported on June 8, 2003, that the Nakornthai Strip Mill company will merge with the Siam Integrated Cold-Rolled Steel company buying up the production machinery from Siam Integrated. TAMC is the major creditor of both companies. NSM company will issue shares to TAMC which in turn will clear debts owed by Siam Integrated. This procedure was approved last year by the Central Bankruptcy Court using a debt-to-equity swap. The result will be steel production will begin for NSM Co. whose capacity of 1.2 million tons per year has been mothballed since 1997 due to the economic crisis.[45]

Other measures are noticed from the same source on August 23, 2003, deputy governor of the Bank of Thailand, Tarisa Watanagasa, announced the central bank was considering various options, which she declined to specify, to help accelerate restructuring of non-performing assets still held by local banks. "The remaining non-performing loans in the system are not a threat to stability, given existing loss provisions. But stripping them out would help local banks operate better."

The International Monetary Fund announced it will close its Thailand office in September, because Thailand has formally graduated from the IMF assistance program in 2000, and completed early repayment of all the loans last month.[46]

Conclusion

Fortuitouslly for Thailand the constitution drafting process coincided with the economic crisis in 1997, and a marvelously devised document was passed through parliament and is being well implemented. Thaksin Shinawatra, the Prime Minister is an excellent administrator and he ahs been willing to accept criticism. I have often commented on the free manner of Thai cartooning even during martial law in the 1970s, it was a clear indication that rigid censorship was not being enforced on Thai press. The active role of the NGOs is remarkable, especially after our creation of VOMPOT during martial law in 1971. There is a real dynamic at work in Thai Society, and Yes, I do feel Thailand has made steady progress toward democracy (Thai style) during these past fifty years, or slightly more than a full generation.

---

45   CF., Bangkok Post, 9 June 2003
46   Bangkok Post, 23 August 2003

Chapter IV

A Return for University Development in Thailand

In January 1971, I discovered that the American involvement in Vietnam was scheduled to be concluded very shortly, and it was time for a return to Thailand. During discussions with retired missionaries I had learned that it was their view that the Thai Government was becoming more inclined to permit the Church of Christ in Thailand to found an institution of higher learning. Our current educational system predated the Thai educational system and we had K-12 education available nationwide for Thai students. For forty years Thai Government officials were saying "No!" to our request to launch an institution of higher learning, and many of those officials were graduates of our educational system. But, official policy from the top Royal level had been a firm "No!" and further, "Look what your institutions did in China, they helped overturn the Government."

Chapter III has shown the tremendous growth of educated Thais now functioning in Bangkok and in many cities across Thailand. Many new educational institutions had been established by Thai Government, and the Ministry of Education was beginning to think more about broadening opportunities. All admission to Thai Government colleges and universities was by competitive examinations and the number of available seats was quite limited. That is, the top 1-2% got admission and the rest were excluded.

What about the rest of those students near the top? No possibilities existed unless the family could send them abroad to study in Europe, Japan, or the United States. It was here in 1971, when I returned to teach for Maryland University (FED) after clearing with Dr. Ray Ehrensberger, University College Chancellor at College Park, and Dr. Joseph Mabbett, Director, Far East Division headquarters in Tokyo that I arrived in Bangkok and took up my assignment at Headquarters, MACTHAI, teaching **Recent Far Eastern Politics,** and met Colonel Raymond F. Ruyffelaere, Comptroller for the MACTHAI Headquarters, who commented, "Mr. Ladd you should found a college." To which I responded, "Do you think it is timely?" and he said, "yes, definitely."

The next week I was in Chiang Mai for a discussion with Dr. E. John Hamlin, Principal of our Thailand Theological Seminary. "Let's have lunch at my house and talk," was his response. Over lunch we discussed the timeliness and his query was, "what can Maryland do for us?" I had no answer, but I would write Dr. Ehrensberger and find out. Dr. Ehrensberger responded that he would like to discuss it when he got out there on his next annual round the world tour of educational centers, Europe, Middle East and Asia. In the fall of 1971, we discussed the possibilities and he went to Chiang Mai for further discussions.

It must be recognized that Maryland University (FED) was never *officially in Thailand*, because Thai law required that all instruction in institutions of higher education must be conducted in Thai language. However, in 1971, UMUC (FED) was teaching at more than ten bases in Thailand. Each of those bases offered classes in Thai language and culture taught by Thai faculty with degrees from , in many cases the United States. More than forty Masters degree and Ph.D.s were teaching with the knowledge of the Ministry of Education. The Minister of

Education at this time was a former Ambassador to the United States, Professor Sukich Nimmanhaeminda, who was a graduate of our Prince Royal's College in Chiang Mai, Thailand. Dr. Ehrensberger never told me what he did, however things began to move. The Ministry was soon willing to discuss curriculum and requested course proposals. By 1973, courses and curriculum content were agreed on. How to launch an institution which needed a physical plant located somewhere with very limited resources, was an issue that needed solution.

The Mission staff was dealing with those issues, and I was in Bangkok teaching. I taught for the Maryland University (FED) program in and near Bangkok during 1971 and 1972. Thailand was under martial law from late in the fall of 1971, and the Thai Government was concerned with the possibility of American forces reducing their presence in Southeast Asia. In December 1971, I was awakened at about 2 AM with a brilliance in my room at the YMCA on Sathorn Tai Road, I glanced out past the Italian Embassy and saw a massive fire burning near the market. I quickly dressed and rushed down the street, and discovered Thai Army trucks packed with people and their belongings parked along the street. The fires were burning their dwellings behind the market where these *squatters* had been living. Shortly the trucks departed and the people were moved out of the city to a country-side site where they were being resettled.

It must have been a week or two later, I was standing in the entranceway of the YMCA residence hall when a group of Catholic Nuns and Fathers entered for an assembly, and Rev. Mr. Maetri Chatrabote, a Thai clergyman I knew came in, and said to me, "come on in with us, Culver." I joined the group of about fifteen people, meeting to hear Sister Matilda, a Thai Nun report on the disappearance of her small squatters' community that she had been nurturing. I mentioned we were under *martial law*, and only five people could legally meet after dusk. Father Johnnie was the convener, a French worker-priest who led the meeting and organized a Volunteer Movement for Peoples Organization in Thailand (VOMPOT) that early evening. He said, "…do not worry about the money, the girls have the money." In essence, when we needed money the Convents in Bangkok had the funds necessary to do the work of helping people. This was an amazing group, and I was the only non-clergy person in it. It consisted of Thai, European and American clergy people, teaching nuns and Mothers-Superior, with Protestants, focusing on the challenges proposed to remove *squatters* across Bangkok.

During the next three years while I was in Bangkok teaching, VOMPOT met many evenings to organize, and ultimately to act to stop the two Field Marshals Thanom and Praphat from carrying out those planned moves. Ultimately, we hired a Thai catholic seminarian from Penang, to carry on the organizing work with two additional Thai field workers. In the Din Daeng *squatters* community a new stadium was being planned and VOMPOT actually organized those squatters to sign petitions and carry them to F.M. Thanom's office and get him to come down and visit; and finally win his acknowledgement that low cost housing was a better solution, than a new stadium. In all those years I was the only American to participate, no Embassy personnel, or International Organization personnel really dared to associate with this creative social action body. It was too politically explosive; our meetings were held in the back assembly rooms in the Convent, where 10 to 20 people regularly gathered challenging the martial law edicts.

In early 1972, I inquired at the International School of Bangkok for daytime teaching and was given many assignments that were quite challenging. ISB in 1972 was very different from the school I had known in 1964-1967. The ISB of 1972 had two sites, and was the largest International School in the world. Johnson's escalation and now Nixon's ventures kept many GIs in combat and their wives and children came to Thailand. These children had **money** and the drug culture had caught them full force!! Ambassador Leonard Unger never fully grasped the significance of this disaster. His policy and the military policy was one of punishment for getting hooked on drugs: **ship the whole family home! That policy was bankrupt from day one!** You have to treat them: or, you create a market in the States. And we have had it ever since!

High school staff pleaded with me to help many of these kids who could not concentrate and were failing. I agreed to tutor them, but not in the afternoons. They must meet me at 6:30 am and Mother must get up and drive them to school. Why, did I do that, because when the children came home in the afternoon Mother was at the Club, and the children were free to get into their own kind of trouble. Now she had to take responsibility to see they got help. Class ran from 6:30 am to 7:25 am and regular ISB classes began at 7:30 am. The transformation was remarkable; kids settled down and grades skyrocketed. But, the key I contend was that the Mother and child were dialoguing.

A Return to Survey Research

In May 1972, Dr. Frederic L. Ayer contacted me and I agreed to come on to his staff to help with a new project he was acquiring. General Motors Corporation was looking at Thailand as a site for future automobile production. Because BRL had data for fifteen years on the socio-economic characteristics in Thailand, we could do a comparative study over that period of time. The issue was: Who can afford to buy General Motors cars and/or trucks? At that time BRL had socio-economic data by household across Bangkok-Thonburi with all classes A through E. Statistically, we could do a random selection of those classes and determine for 1972, those who were capable of buying such vehicles. We designed that study to measure the potential for Thailand, and fielded it with interviewers who were university students in their school uniforms. Those interviewers were so respected by Thais that we could depend on honest answers.

The outcome of the report I wrote was that Thais were capable of buying automobiles and were interested in Classes A,B,C, and even in Class D. The extended family is the "key" to buying important items in Thai cultural thinking; reasonable loans can be arranged within the "family." With information of that sort, General Motors began to move swiftly, and it was in early 1974, that I was invited to the opening ceremony for BangChan Automotive Corporation's new factory. We were shown a splendid new assembly plant: General Motors had entered into its first "triple;" Alpha Romero, Volkswagen, and General Motors Chevrolet Division from Australia with cars and pick-up trucks. That initial success has multiplied again and again, now in 2006, the **pick-up truck** is the largest vehicle output from General Motors operations in Thailand and with exports as its focus in Southeast Asia.

Monsoon Drainage Systems

In the years I had been back in the States, 1967-1970, my colleague Linne Tholin had been busy, and his engineering contribution was recognized by leading Thais and he was asked to act as an advisor to the Lord mayor of Bangkok. In the Monsoon Season in Bangkok the heavy rains actually flooded the city; main streets could be one and a half to two feet under water. Minor *klongs* along the streets, Sukhumvit, Wireless Road, and Rama IV Road had been put into underground drainage pipes and now interconnected to a large eight-foot diameter pipe form Klong Toey to Rama IV Road. This massive pipe had been built by Welch miners tunneling up from Klong Toey to Rama IV Road. At Klong Toey was a cylindrical chamber from surface to 75 feet below ground, where four massive pumps were located to drain that entire center city and pump it out into the Chao Phraya River.

Fresh Water for a Growing City

So successful was this venture that Bangkok entered into World Bank proposals for a new underground fresh water system for the city. When I returned in 1971, Linne was in the midst of this design, drawing upon that vast experience in Chicago, he was doing the sort of creative work that he truly loved! When I called upon him in his office he showed me his drawings and explained how the water lines would feed the communities of the city of Bangkok. Along some of those lines he had drawn *his proposed subway lines.* One must live in Bangkok and drive in Bangkok to understand the cultural complexities which affect traffic: and Linne knew them and understood that a subway might well be the only way to surmount cultural difficulties. In July 2004 that Subway opened its first stages across Bangkok difficulties.

I am citing these two ***vitally important proposals because they clash so directly with Thai cultural values.*** Hindu-Buddhist philosophy teaches three levels of existence: the Lords in the Heavens; Human existence on earth; and the world of the Devil below ground. These two proposals and then as projects: Drainage Systems, and a Subway, are directly contradictory to the dominant philosophy. There is also a history of cultural rejection: when I left Thailand in September 1975, I had to wade in flood waters in Bangkok over my knees. As long as Linne Tholin was in Thailand, the pumps worked; however, he retired to Hawaii in late 1974; and I understand that the flooding continued until 1978 when the King intervened and ordered "…turn those pumps on!" Similarly, a near thirty year battle raged over the subway, which was authorized in 1976, but met constant rejection for cultural reasons; the magnificent subway opened in July 2004.[47]

This has been a look at a fifty year transition for the Thai people, as we educated their bureaucracy and their university faculties; and as these leaders accepted new ideas and then implemented them in their own ways. It is a direct contrast to the nation adjacent to the west, Burma, has rejected change and is struggling with internal conflicts of ethnic groups that should have been rallied to be more Burmese. The Thais

---

47 *BangkokPost.com*, August 2, 2006, "Cabinet gives nod for three subway lines."

have been willing to make changes and Burmese have lacked that ability for a complex of reasons.

A Look at the Need for Steel

In 1973, I undertook a study of the need for *steel castings* for Mitsui Corporation of Japan, and that took me into industrial sites across lower Thailand. Fire hydrants, brake shoes, railroad junction boxes, and pipe fittings and import statistics all were where I ventured. I importantly talked to the engineers planning the water system now financed by the World Bank, and found, "No, the pipes were not steel." "Pipes will be concrete, because Thailand makes the worlds' best concrete." However, the valves would be steel castings.

In my drives in Thailand south of Bangkok and along the Gulf of Siam I was struck by a row of six or eight massive steel tanks, and inquired what they contained. "Corn Syrup, was the answer to my great surprise." A super-tanker would periodically anchor at an outlet in the Gulf and pump dry these tanks and transport the corn syrup to canneries in Hong Kong, Japan, or Taiwan for fruit packing, and beverage bottling. Not many castings here, but this realization opened up a whole industry in corn processing I had not understood was developing in Thailand. We Americans had introduced *Guatemala Corn* to Thailand and educated Thai and Chinese chemists were transforming that agricultural product into an industrial product undergirding the Thai economy. Glucose production has achieved such a level of proficiency that medical grade glucose is being produced for hospital usage. Automotive plants, textile weaving plants, bottling plants and breweries all use some castings, and yet the import statistics were the best data for the steel castings study.

The USOM-Thailand Contract

Beginning mid-summer 1973 I was asked by Dr. Robert Zimmerman, Research Director of USOM-Thailand to work in the Training Division of USOM to evaluate the computerization of Thai Training Records from the start in 1950 to current conditions. Together with a Thai assistant working in that division we clarified the record which had been kept by a separate office of the Thai Ministry in cooperation with USOM. The paper records were all kept under lock and key in USOM offices, it was the record keeping by the Thai Ministry which became such a challenge. As we worked with the paper records in correcting the computer record it became clearly evident that many senior military and administrative officials' training records were simply missing from the computer records. This project far exceeded the estimated time we had projected to complete this work and we worked late into the evenings for months. The final product literally transformed the process of planning, costing, and administering the training division. Working under the supervision of Mr. Herbert Roberts, we had modernized the Training Division operations in Bangkok and he later took those concepts more broadly within the AID missions world-wide.

Valves, and More Valves

All of our computer work was being done by an American-run regional computer office for most of East Asia established to service Embassies in Southeast Asian countries located in Bangkok. With that level of competence we were able to accomplish significant changes of product for managements' use. On several occasions while computer work was being run I had time to return to work with Business Research Co., Ltd.; and on one of those occasions, Dr. Ayer confronted me with a problem they had met with the Thai engineering supervisor for contracting on the Water System being built for Bangkok. He could not tell them how many valves would be needed for the system. I went down and asked him, and he could not tell me either. So with the help of my colleague, Amnuay, I found an engineer with an American Engineer's Handbook and with careful use of a set of tables, I projected the valves needed by size and their numbers and wrote a concise report. Within a year thereafter, my colleagues reported with compliments on the accuracy of that report from Japanese concerns involved in the construction activities related to the Water System.

Infant Food Study

In April of 1974, Dr. Zimmerman contacted me regarding the possibility of fielding a study into high protein infant foods produced in Thailand. The Thais cook a lot of very tasty food; but studies have shown that infant Thais are feed rice as an infant food. In Thai cultural settings rice must be *polished white rice, i.e.,* with the protein layers removed. Only prisoners are fed brown rice with the husk remaining. Therefore, after weaning, growth is stunted; a high protein infant food was highly desirable. There was no food manufacturing in Thailand; we reached out to the most prominent restaurateur in Bangkok with linkages to Thai Farmers Bank and won their interest. Coordinating with food chemists at Kasetasrt University, we found a very tasty and easy on the tongue pabulum which they had devised. These Thai worked to begin a food manufacturing operation in Bangkok; this food manufacturing effort evolved into Tofu production and it has flourished ever since.

Payap College Opens Its Doors

By May 1974, the planning process for Payap College had achieved curriculum approval from the Ministry of Education and the dormitory for Christian students at the Crystal Spring House for Chiang Mai University students was converted to classrooms for our use when we opened classes in June 1974. Faculty was hired, and students had been tested and selection was complete. Tuition had been paid and students who had been excluded from higher education began their studies at the new Payap College. Our oldest freshman student was a 32 year old woman who was now earning her bachelor degree planning to be a teacher. Our total enrollment that first semester was 204 students.

The critically important document for opening was the Thai Ministry of Education certificate of physical facilities, issued for our June 1974 opening. The converted dormitory conveyed by the Church of Christ in Thailand to Payap College's Board of Directors was that physical facility, a total of six classrooms. The second dormitory was never converted to classrooms because students at Chiang Mai University were still living there. At noon we transported students across the city of Chiang Mai to the McCormick Hospital's Nursing School classrooms for afternoon classes. The Nursing School had adjusted their schedule and had morning classes including laboratory classes and went into the hospital for afternoon ward work; here we had three floors of classrooms.

The three faculties in Chiang Mai that wanted a four year college established were: the McCormick School of Nursing, Midwifery, and Public Health; the Thailand Theological Seminary; and the School of Church Music. Theology had been taught in Chiang Mai from the 1890s, Nursing was begun in 1923, and Church Music was recent in the 1960s. Now the possibility of graduate level education was created.

June 22, 1974 marked the formal dedication of Payap College, with the Deputy Prime Minister, formerly the Minister of Education and Ambassador to the United States, Dr. Sukich Nimmanhaeminda, representing the Thai Government, charging the faculty and administration to thoroughly educate the many Thai students, who would enroll in Payap College.

As its growth has shown, Payap College history is testimony to the need for private education in Thailand. In 1984, Payap filed for university status and Payap University became the first private university in Thailand. In 2006 Payap University offers more than 24 bachelor degree programs, three master's degree programs, and enrolls students from 23 countries around the world. Thai students can now enroll in a special 2 + 2 bachelor degree program in Chinese from Payap University and Southwest University (in Chongqing, China).

Chapter V

Funding the University's Development

In September 1975, I left Thailand for an academic experience in England. I had applies to St Antony's College, Oxford University, and they had inquired about me in Thailand and then declined my request. And so I stopped for a week in Bangkok before flying to Europe. I had brought a library of books to Thailand to teach with Maryland and now was shipping them to the States. In all the flood waters in Chiang Mai and now in Bangkok this was quite a challenge. There was no reason for this flood in Bangkok, but of course, Linne Tholin was gone in retirement to Hawaii.

I stopped to talk briefly with Rev. Dr. Horace Ryburn, our head of Presbyterian Missions and explained what I was trying to do. He had some straight forward advice: go talk to the British Counsel offices, and explain what you want to do. And, so I did, told that young woman that I hoped to study at Oxford or Cambridge and she suggested some other school maybe, and I said no, I had visited Oxford years ago with my parents and was quite interested in studying there.

And by the end of the week I was packed and shipped and aboard a Swiss Air Charter flight to Zurich. My assigned seat put me with a family from the Philippines, Dr. and Mrs. Paul Lauby, who were leaving

Silliman University and headed to offices in New York City. We talked on that long non-stop flight and in Zurich, Dr. Lauby suggested that I come to see him in New York when I did get back to the States; and I agreed to do so.

On the surface from Zurich to London with five bags including a typewriter made for tough movement. I checked most of the baggage in London and went out to Oxford to inquire about enrolling. At the registrars office he was expecting me, and I was assigned a reader, and an advisor. Paul P. Streeten was my reader, and I knew him by name, as I was a member of the Society for International Development, and Paul regularly wrote for them; but he was from Sussex and now I found him at Oxford. My advisor, was the Gladstone Professor of All Soul's College, Oxford, Samuel E. Finer, chairman of Social Studies for Oxford University. I was told to talk with my advisor first and when I suggested a topic for my study, he added a few words, "…considered in the Light of the Experience of Third World Countries Generally." I said, "gosh, that will take me a whole year." And it did! He also insisted I include Iraq in my study. And IRAQ is in the study and in the final doctoral dissertation as well.

With two men of this caliber I was completely absorbed in the academic process, and with Professor Finer's guidance to "take all the seminars you find interesting," I was present in 12 to 15 seminars each term at Oxford. Seminars in 1975-76 were eight lectures long, except for the class Professor Finer taught, which ran for 16 lectures, Participants were told that the faculty was available to meet them when ever they were ready to have a further discussion of the work a student was pursuing. Many students then left England to do field work in the region or country of their research interest. It was this kind of study that I had had with Dr. William Y. Elliott at American University in 1964. He had polished that method of working with students since his years at Oxford as a Rhodes Scholar.

The paper I worked to research and integrate with experiences in Thailand won the title: THE EVOLUTION OF FORMS OF GOVERNMENT AS THE CONSTITUTIONAL LAW MATURES AND THE ECONOMY OF THE STATE MOVES TOWARD INTERDEPENDENCE WITH THE DEVLOPED COUNTRIES, WITH SPECIAL REFERENCE TO THE COUNTRY OF THAILAND CONSIDERED IN THE LIGHT OF THE EXPERIENCES OF THIRD WORLD COUNTRIES GENERALLY. There you can see I was integrating the political philosophy of Constitutionalism knit together with the economic development I had witnessed in Thailand over the decade of the 1960s and 1970s.

Oxford was so uniquely different form my American educational experiences, I was truly captivated and inspired to excel. Studies in the Asian study center probing deeply into Japanese history, Middle Eastern Seminars, Latin American Seminars, and Economic Development Seminars, all at my finger tips gave me unique insights. Oxford has the Bodleian Library and many other libraries across the campus; it is truly a great institution for research scholars.

My 213 page treatise was bound and rendered to my reader, Professor Paul P. Streeten in late April 1976, and I returned to the States in May 1976. My flight was non-stop from Luxemburg directly to Miami, Florida; and while attending Church in Coral Gables I learned that the Presbyterians were meeting in their General Assembly in Baltimore next week. My parents assisted me with a Chevrolet and I loaded my boxes of books and drove to Washington, and then to Baltimore in search of Dr. Paul Lauby. Staff of the General Assembly I knew assured me Dr. Lauby was in New York in the offices of the United Board for Christian Higher Education in Asia. I drove on to New York City and call the next morning and arranged to meet with him in his office.

Over a cup of tea, we discussed Payap College and its future in

Thailand together with a discussion of my work at Oxford University. Then Dr.Lauby said he had just received $400,000 for a Library at Silliman University. "How did you do that?" He discussed the way he had arranged to apply for the funds, and I took careful note of how he had succeeded. And then I went back to Washington and went to work. It might be well to say that my grandfather had been a United States Senator in the 1920s and I have always felt quite at home on Capital Hill. Senator Milton Young had taught me something about persistence, when he related how my Uncle, D. Milton Ladd had negotiated the FBI Retirement Bill through the Congress. My task was now to negotiate with a senator from Hawaii, Senator Daniel K. Inouye, and repeated visits got me literally nowhere. On the fourth visit I arrived just after Elizabeth Taylor had left, she had caused quite a stir of that staff, and when I inquired of the Senator I was told yes he was in and I went in to see him. We had a brief exchange and I asked if he thought a college in Thailand might qualify for financial assistance. He thought for a while and said, "Well we have put a lot of money into the Middle East and yes, we might well consider some in Southeast Asia." He gave me the name of an official in USAID, State Department, and I left for a visit to AID. That official provided me with the necessary application forms and they were sent by airmail to Dr. Konrad Kingshill, Payap College, Chiang Mai, Thailand. Konrad's initial request was for slightly less than two million dollars, for surveying, grading and for filling low lands to lift buildings above the flood plains. State Department engineers participated in this process to be assured that the college was being built right.

It took a year or more for the Congress to appropriate the funds, and finally construction could begin. It is important to note that in Thailand all upland areas are owned by the Royal Purse and managed by the Privy Council. Payap could not acquire lands on Approaches to the mountain areas, and had to buy lowland areas previously used for rice planting. Thus, we were confronted by the need to lift ground levels and channel flood waters away from our buildings. The campus at Mae Khao, outside the beltway east of Chiang Mai, is a marvel of interconnected buildings with covered walkways to protect during monsoon storms. Students can pass from class to class without getting wet and be on time for their next lecture. The ten to twelve million dollars spent on Payap buildings and other aspects of engineering have completed twenty-five or more multi-story classroom buildings and administrative offices. Money carefully spent goes a long way in Thailand.

> A recent letter from the retiring President of Payap University highlights this development: "(W)e just completed construction of our new central library this past year, affectionately named the **Sirindhorn Learning Resource Center.** The library is named after the Princess of Thailand, a highly respected and nationally adored figure. Princess Sirindhorn presided over our opening ceremony in October 2005 and was extremely impressed by the facility. This library, partially funded by the American Schools and Hospitals Abroad (ASHA) and the US Agency for International Development (USAID), is an architectural marvel. It's equipped with some of the most advanced and technologically sophisticated learning resources available. In summary, this facility contains over 400 persoanl computers for student use, private student study rooms, four auditoriums equipped with state-of-the-art audio/visual equipment, various lounges and study areas, student entertainment centers, a Northern Thai learning center, millions of pages of books in paper and digital format, and an historical museum which chronicles our university's humble beginnings. Needless to say, we are quite proud of this library and believe that it will serve as an invaluable learning resource for our students and faculty for many years to come"[48]

---

48 Boonthong Poocharoen, Ph.D., "Message from the President of Payap University, "April 2006.

Dr. Poocharoen also highlighted the significant faculty development program which has now produced five new nursing instructors with PhDs. A brand new graduate/doctorate program will be introduced beginning in 2006-2007 academic year. These nurses will be part of that program looking toward meeting severe shortages in nurses in Thailand and abroad.

The Payap University Law School program in making Thai history, as in its recent case which reached the Thai Supreme Court winning citizenship for 1,200 northern people who were stateless and suffering abuse and neglect. The Business Incubator program (PYUBI) is encouraging students to start their own businesses, and provides consultation and guidance; with business ideas in computer networking, animation and graphic design, music, and accounting.

If you take your map of Asia and look for Chiang Mai, Thailand, you notice its interesting position up close to China, not too far from Bangladesh, and India. It is connected by international airways and that makes it an ideal location for international conferences. June 24-30, 2007, Payap University's Institute for the Study of Religion and Culture, is co-sponsoring an International Conference on **"Religion and Culture."** When you realize the other sponsors include: the American Society for Buddhist-Christian Studies, Harvard University's Center for the Study of World Religions, ASIA Network, International Network of Engaged Buddhists, AMAN (Asian Muslim Action Network), Church of Christ in Thailand, Asian Christian higher Education Institute, The Christian Conference of Asia (CCA), and the Philosophy and Religion Society of Thailand, you understand that Payap University is engaged in the most critically important dialogue in the world of the twenty-first century.

The Conference will coincide with the publication of the Thai translation of H. Richard Niebuhr's *Christ and Culture.* Keynote presentations and panels will focus on the relation of religion and culture from inter-religious and cross-cultural perspectives. Speakers and panelists will include leading international scholars from Buddhist, Christian, East Asian, Hindu, Islamic, Modern Tribal and Secular traditions. Speakers will represent a variety of academic fields and disciplines, including the comparative study of religion, the history of religion, the study of particular religious communities, theology, and the social sciences.[49]

Here we see the atheistic Chinese and the violence of the Middle East confronted rationally in pure academic dialogue where they are afraid to confront their ethnic and cultural values for reasoned discussion and possible solutions.

---

49   http://isrc.payap.ac.th

Chapter VI

Thailand Stumbles, Recovers and Is Growing: Asia and the World Are Watching.

In the mid-1990s the world was watching Hong Kong with intensity as Britain negotiated with Communist China; when you realize that many of the businessmen in Bangkok were former KMT Chinese now in leading positions in industry and finance in Thailand, in their perspective Bangkok offered a logical site for many Hong Kong Chinese businessmen if they wanted to move to a new location in Asia. You may recall that Canada was offering a similar option.

My visit to Bangkok in 1987, revealed significant growth, with as many as forty buildings of the **tall building style,** which I viewed from the 24th floor of the Chokechai Building. However, by 1997, investors had begun a massive building program and were apparently risking everything on an illusion: Hong Kong business fleeing China.

The 1997 Economic Crisis

Thailand may well have begun it, but it affected Korea, Taiwan, Japan and China, and others in Southeast Asia. Thailand had linked its currency, the baht to the US dollar at 20 to 1. The Ministry of Finance announced the currency would *float;* actually in time it assumed a rate of 43 to 1 with the US dollar. A sharp devaluation of currency in Thailand, well known for its *hard currency,* and steel tycoon Sawasdi Horrungruang issued a defiant, "No money, no pay, and no flee," which made headlines in Bangkok. NPL is the essential phrase for Thailand's crisis: "non-performing loans."[50]

Many buildings completed, but without occupants, little or no research for alternatives, and banks holding NPLs spelled financial crisis. Call it a class reunion of sorts, with several hundred top industrialists gathered together to swap stories about how they fended off creditors and lawyers, secured new partners and generally survived the 1997 economic crisis.[51] Ucom in 2000 was forced to sell a major stake to Norway's Telenor to help restructure its debts. General agreement among a broad array of companies in the steel, construction, and property sectors, agreed that the crisis imparted important lessons about the need for prudent financial management, risk controls, and diversified markets.

Due to the financial crisis Thailand accepted a US$17.2 billion standby credit program from the International Monetary Fund in 1997, after having exhausted the country's foreign reserves in a failed effort to support the currency. And in typical Thai fashion, the country exited from the IMF program in 2000. Repayment of all loans from the IMF and other creditors was completed ahead of schedule.

Mr. Horst Kohler, managing director of the International Monetary Fund, commented during an interview with the Bangkok Post, "the Thai economy was recovering well, with fiscal policy moving toward prudential consolidation…structural reforms in the banking system should also be pushed forward, given the continued high rate of non-performing loans."[52]

---

50 *Bangkok Post*, July 3, 2003, "Baht Devaluation: Six Years On."
51 *Ibid.*
52 *Bangkok Post.*, September 7, 2003, "APEC FINANCE MINISTERS: Kohler uges cautionary spending."

Politics Spelled: Thai Rak Thai Party

The Election of January 2001 elected 248 seats only three shy of an overall majority, for Mr. Thaksin Shinawatra's Thai Rak Thai Party. Fourteen MPs of Seritham Party merged with TRT so that a solid majority now ruled the Parliament. Prime Minster Thaksin tried to assert his policies on all issues and in early 2003, acting through the Foreign Ministry overseas non-governmental organizations were to be asked to stop funding dissident NGOs targeting the Assembly for the Poor, the NGO handling problems concerning the Pak Moon dam, and the Thai Volunteer Service;[53] but, the Foreign Ministry turned him down.

It should be noted that PM Thaksin is reputedly the holder of a Texas Ph.D. in Security Management and is a Thai police colonel; he is also the fourth wealthiest man in Thailand.[54] His critics' biggest concerns are the combination of wealth and political power, and the risk that he might use one to advance the other. There is no denying that a company controlled by his family bought up Thailand's only private television channel and subsequently fired many of its free-thinking reporters.[55]

PM Thaksin spoke to his TRT Party faithful, saying, "The scenario is clear. Other parties will be preoccupied with fighting for their own survival and they should not even contemplate a victory over Thai Rak Thai…People may talk endlessly about how much the government has achieved. Unlike ours, previous administrations' achievements ran out even before you finished your coffee." He envisaged Thai Rak Thai retaining its grip on power for at least 20 more years.[56]

Thirayuth Boonmi, lecturer at Thammasat University, speaking

---

53 *Bangkok Post*, May 8, 2003, "SILENCING THE CRITICS: PM tried to cut funds to NGOs."
54 *Bangkok Post*, July 18, 2006, citing *Forbes Asia*, July 24, 2006 edition.
55 *The Economist*, March 2, 2002, "A Survey of Thailand."
56 *Bangkok Post*, April 28, 2003, "TRT set for 20 years in power."

at the 30th anniversary of the October 14, 1973 Student Uprising, lashed out at the government, saying Prime Minister Thaksin Shinawatra was putting the country at risk with his populist policies and authoritarian tendencies. "With Thaksin's "CEO style, the people will be more greedy. There is no sin but stupidity, no pride but profit , and no morality but money."[57]

---

57 *Bangkok Post, October 6, 2003, "Thaksin putting Thailand, 'at risk'"*

Abandoned Construction Project after mass relocation from Hong Hong did not materialize after China took control. Numerous sites like this throughout Bangkok.

Thailand's First Completed Parliamentary Term: Thaksin's Way

Thaksin Shinawatra, a tycoon-turned-politician, has survived a complete four year term without a coup. It causes an observer to note the only prior occasion was when Kriangsak Chomanan, a Thai coup leader, resigned from that office in 1980 taking a democratic step of resigning rather than being overthrown, telling the parliament that he felt he no longer had public support.[58]

The Thai economy has made dramatic improvements during this four year term, in 2001 the economy grew only 2.1%, in 2003 the economy grew by 6.8% and in 2004 it grew by 6.2%. Many of his supporters give Thaksin high credit for using business acumen to lead the nation forward. His policies of medical care for just 30 baht (75 cents) per consultation, debt relief for farmers, and micro-credit for villagers has proved so popular that the Democrat Party is copying many of these ideas. On the whole, these innovations have helped to make Thai politics more responsive to the concerns of ordinary voters, and less dependent on the whims of backroom politicians.

Thaksin bought up bad debts of state-owned banks so that they could resume lending, and then forced them to do so. Thai economists have been fearful that this wholesale pump-priming, though effective, would end up bankrupting the government.[59] Ideally, an opposition, Democrat Party, would act as a check and balance, but, it was unlikely that the election in 2005 would help check him.

Opposition Grows

Thailand's opposition parties won three of the four contested parliamentary seats in a by-election on Sunday, giving them sufficient

---

58 *The Economist,* January 10, 2004. Obituary.
59 *Ibid.,* February 5, 2005, Thaksin's Way.

seats to launch a no-confidence motion against the cabinet. Opposition parties now hold 126 seats in the 500 seat parliament, sufficient to launch a no-confidence motion, though unlikely to win such a vote of no confidence.[60] Thaksin's CEO style of managing government is beginning to earn criticism and he now responds, "I have surveyed people's opinions all along and found they are still happy with the government's performance. I won't be shameless staying on in office unless people want my government."[61]

Popular talk-show host Sondhi Limthongkul, of a government-run television station was cancelled in September 2005, and began a series of Lumpini park rallies as a substitute, gathering tens of thousands to hear his criticisms of PM Thaksin and his government. Mr. Sondhi has unveiled fresh allegations of official corruption and misconduct, while the prime minister has filed repeated law suits for libel. Despite denials, Sondhi claims – the government ferried guests to Mr. Thaksin's sister's birthday party on an air force plane, padded the purchase price for luggage scanners for the new International Airport, and usurped the prerogatives of the country's Buddhist patriarch.[62]

On February 4, 2006, chief organizer Sondhi Limthongkul, convened the largest rally of protest outside the royal palace to demand the Prime Minister's resignation. The protester were to wear or carry something *yellow*, a color with royal and Buddhist connotations but also to deliberately to echo the "color revolutions" of the Ukraine and elsewhere. Estimates ran as high as 100,000 protesters, and they called for impeachment proceedings.

The January sale by the Shinawatra family of its Shin Corporation controlling stake in the telecom and media empire may have been hope to ease the pressure on Thaksin, but it has only intensified. Now it has emerged that the prime ministerial clan used a loophole in the tax laws

---

60   *Bangkok Post*, October 31, 2005, Thailand election update.
61   *Ibid.*, November 30, 2005.
62   *The Economist*, December 17, 2005, "The oracle of Lumpini park."

(albeit a legal one) to avoid tax on the nearly $2 billion transaction; these concerns gave the anti-Thaksin rallies new momentum.[63]

Privy Council chairman Prem Tinsulanonda had expressed concerns about morals and ethics in leadership in a lecture reported by the media, PM Thaksin felt it wise to call upon this important personage at his Si Sao Theves residence. An issue raised was the presence of chairman's former secretary, Maj-Gen Chamlong Srimuang at the PAD rally.[64]

The People's Alliance for Democracy (PAD) has formed to make formal protest of Thaksin's Rules. Pol. Maj-Gen. Chamlong Srimuang, Sondhi Limthongkul, Pipop Thongchai, Somsak Kosaisuk and Somkiart Pongpaiboon organized PAD to lead street protest, and the three main opposition parties were prompted to boycott the snap election called by the Prime Minister for April 2, 2006. The dissolution of the House of Representative in March created a caretaker government. The boycott by the opposition parties spelled the defeat of the TRT effort to win parliamentary control and the King acted to order the Courts to "solve this mess."

The result has been political bedlam, yet the celebration of the King's 60th year of reign went off smoothly, with royalty from around the world in attendance.

Thailand's Functioning Bureaucracy

I have previously discussed in Chapter III the education and training efforts of USOM-Thailand over the period 1950-1975, resulting in trained bureaucrats an absolutely fundamental requirement for a modern government in the twenty-first century. In the two to three decades USOM trained Thais we equipped the nation to succeed developmentally. The majority of those trained bureaucrats are in Bangkok,

---

63 *Ibid.*, February 11, 2006, "Thaksin's yellow peril."
64 *Bangkok Post*, February 9, and February 24, 2006, "Embattled PM sees Prem."

and form the vast middle class for that society. These are the socially conscious and politically active who are responding to Thaksin's Rule.

Ministry of Energy

In early 2003, the Ministry was discussing a Kra Isthmus canal, again after 40 years. This would cut through the essentially Muslim states of South Thailand. They were also wrestling with the concept of Thailand being the center of power transmission for the states of Southeast Asia. Because power generation in Burma would be half the cost of Thai generation, the Salween River Dam was discussed from the perspective of financing either by state agencies with private partners or by EGAT alone, with the Burmese government. By the end of the year, Burma and Thailand were calling upon China to clarify its plans to build multiple dams on the Salween in Yunnan province. On March 1, 2006, Egat Plc. Would only reveal that "It is expected the first dam, with 1,000-megawatt generating capacity, will be built 50 km deep into Burmese territory opposite Tak province within two years."[65]

At about the same time, EGAT was asking Laos to clarify its plans for a Nam Theun 2 Dam for hydropower to be delivered to Thailand. EGAT was also under intense pressure to corporatize to raise 60 billion baht with IPO scheduled for March 2004. It was announced that Egat would hold a roadshow in New York at JP Morgan's annual investors' meeting from Sept. 29 to Oct. 1.[66] However, employees of EGAT led strikes and protests which resulted in Court actions and in March 2006, the Supreme Administrative Court ruled against the government's privatization plans for Egat Plc. The state owned electricity company. It said that Orlarn Chaipravat, a board member of Shin Corp. which is a business partner of Egat, was on the committee laying the groundwork for the privatization. The court questioned the neutrality of Parinya

---

65 *Bangkok Post*, January 23, 2003, December 18, 2003, "China plans 13 dams on Salween;" and March 1, 2006.
66 *Ibid.*, Sept. 16, 2003, "EGAT."

Nutalai, chair of the public hearing panel on the Egat listing, because he was an assistant to the natural resources and environment minister. The Court also ruled that Egat had not yet handed over the tracts of public land that were expropriated by the government to the state. Based on these facts, the Court found the corporatization process illegal and ordered the two decrees (underpinning the privatization) repealed.[67]

By 2005, Nam Theun 2 is financed and started with the foundation stone laid. Lao authorities tell Thailand they will supply 3,849 MW from seven plants into the Thai national grid at any time to benefit both Thai and Lao people.[68]

Ministry of Transportation

The transformation of automobile manufacturing in Thailand since the BRL 1972 study has been dramatic. "We are aiming to become the biggest pickup truck player in Thailand," said William Botwick, President and managing director of GM (Thailand).[69] His new Rayong plant now produces since the 1997 crisis, Chevrolet Zafira multi-purpose vehicle, Chevrolet Optra mid-range sedan and a pickup truck model for Isuzu, GM's affiliate, only for export. The Zafira is exported to 19 countries and the Optra, which only started to be produced in July 2003, is shipped to Indonesia, the Philippines and Malaysia.

"Why is Bangkok the place for pickups?" It is the world's second-largest producer of pickup trucks after America. Investment is pouring in, in 2003 Ford unveiled plans to spend $500 million to expand production. Nissan, having forked out $190 million to increase its stake in a joint venture is now investing another $250 million on new assembly lines. Toyota is spending $750 million to set up a research and

---

67 *Ibid.*, March 23, 2006, "Court quashes Egat listing."
68 *Ibid.*, January 30, 2006, "Lao power deal imminent."
69 *Bangkok Post*, October 16, 2003, "GM to beef up plant, add pickups."

development center. Mitsubishi has even found $525 million to invest in its booming Thai operations.[70]

While Thailand struggled with *cultural issues* on a subway, German engineers convinced the transportation decision-makers to build an elevated rail system known as the **Skytrain**. This impressive third floor train traverses ten miles of the business centers of Bangkok, and finally in 2004, it is beginning to break even financially.[71]

Road building had a high importance in the era 1965-1976, during the Vietnam Conflict, since five straight miles of level paved road, was an excellent emergency land strip. Thailand came to realize their lignite coal deposits were the key to improved road surfacing. Today Thailand has excellent road literally from border to border, and they are used by domestic and international tourists in air-conditioned buses, trucks carrying cargo from fields to processing plants and to markets, and increasingly for inter-country travel. Earlier this year, Thailand opened its second bridge into Burma at Baan Sanpakhi, in Chiang Rai Province, to support Chiang Rai's special economic zone development, on the route to China.[72]

Shippers complain of high border fees in the current route to China, and Thailand is speeding up negotiations with China on a third bridge across the Mekong River (two bridges exist at Vientiane, Laos) at Chiang Kong to Baan Huay Sai. The current negotiations on bridge construction, focuses on the Thai desire for Chinese sharing the budget in the same amount.[73]

---

70 *The Economist*, September 11, 2004, "Motown in Thailand."
71 *Bangkok Post*, December 1, 2004, BTSC announces improved ridership.
72 *Ibid.*, January 22, 2006, "Thailand, Burma open second bridge."
73 *Ibid.*, June 8, 2006, "New Mekong bridge to link Thailand-China."

Thailand Transformed: 1950-2012

Subtleties of the struggle to build a subway in Thailand: Linne Tholin's 1972 drawings for the water system funded by the World Bank (IBRD) for Metropolitan Bangkok included *proposed subway lines*. All of this underground work violates the Hindu-Buddhist tenets not to enter into the *world of the Devil!* It must be understood that Thai Ministry buildings are in majority built on the land of Buddhist religious organizations. Ministries usually front on major streets, and directly behind them are the respective *Wats* of that religious sect. It is expected that the *Minister* will consult with the *Head Abbot* in the daily course of business. Thus, when the Minister of Transportation broaches the idea of a **subway** the Abbot properly suggests it is not wise to build such a structure.

This should explain why it took twenty-eight years from the 1976 decision to plan to build a subway until it is in fact functioning in 2004. The struggle is one of over-coming basic cultural barriers. The fact that this subway is now carrying major Thai work force daily is quiet testimony to the wisdom of the transportation leaders and the quiet encouragement of the King of Thailand.

So successful has been the subway in Bangkok that three new mass transit subway lines were given the go-ahead with funding to be arranged both domestically and overseas. The three lines were considered urgent as they would help ease traffic and save the traveling public time. They are the 40 km Red Line from Phya Thai to Rangsit and Chiang Rak Noi; the 23 km Purple Line from Bang Yai to Bang Sue; and the current subway route, the Blue Line, to be lengthened 14 km from Hua Lamphong to Bang Khae and by 13 km from Bang Sue to Tha Phra. The Red Line will connect with the new International Airport Link train to Suvarnabhumi airport, currently being tested.[74]

---

74 *Bangkok Post*, July 30, 2006, "All systems go for historic Suvarnabhumi flights today," August 2, 2006, "Cabinet gives nod for three subway lines."

Ministry of Industry and Ministry of Agriculture

These are two ministries staffed with highly skilled bureaucrats. The Prime Minister's goal of making Thailand, the "World's Kitchen" by making sure export produce was free of chemical residues and diseases, led to his urging them to upgrade the standards for produce consumed locally.[75] Kasetsart University, the National Innovation Agency (NIA), and the Federation of Thai Industries coordinating with the Phetchabun Province rice producers have embraced the challenge of increasing the price-setting power of Thai rice exporters within a fiercely competitive global market. The strategy is to sell brown rice which has been orizinized: Orizination begins with putting rice grains in water until they reach the saturation point. The grains then undergo a heating process until they are semi-cooked. Finally, they are blow-dried. Brown rice produced from this technique is superior to other processed brown rice because it retains all of the vitamins and minerals that occur naturally in rice germ and bran.[76]

In the early 1960s in Thailand, milk was simply not available unless you were an Indian family who kept one or two cows for their milk. Electricity was not constant and therefore no refrigeration existed. With Yanhee power in December 1964, refrigeration became a possibility for Thai families generally. In traveling up-country in the 1970s it was amazing to see workers in the fields cutting grass and feeding cows. Today, milk and milk products, yogurt and ice creams are readily available and the Thai diet has made remarkable changes. "We saw huge potential to expand our business in this region because dairy consumption has more than tripled from 15 years ago. In Thailand, alone, consumption is only 20 million liters, compared to 58 million in Singapore and 140 million in European countries.[77]

Largely because of *Avian Flu* shrimp production is looking to

---

75   *Ibid.*, March 11, 2003, "Better food safety for all next year."
76   *Ibid.*, January 23, 2006, "Superior brown rice could help market."
77   *Ibid.*, January 27, 2006, "Milk firms pool resources."

expand exponentially, with the major expansion in production capacity, revenue from shrimp would exceed those from chicken within three years,[78] in a CPF "bio-secure" plant. Viya Crab Products Co. of Surat Thani aims to extend its export business to increase revenue, with ready-to-eat pasteurized canned blue crab meat. Well established in local markets and with a broker handling US marketing, Viya Products is looking especially at European and Asian markets, with help from the Department of Export Promotion.[79]

Another area of significant industrial development is the petroleum industry, and PPT Exploration and Production Plc, a PPT subsidiary, has been upgraded to AAA, the highest rating attained by any company in Thailand, from AA+ assigned by Tris Rating.[80] PTT insists it is a state enterprise with key investments to be made in the petrochemical manufacturing facilities, oil refinery capacity expansion, and gas separation plants. Anti-Thaksin and anti-privatisation groups have alleged that huge benefits in the form of capital gains and dividends from PPT stock had gone to a handful of major shareholders, who happen to be related to politicians of the Thai Rak Thai Party.[81] Thus, we see the Prime Minister with his hand in many projects, much like a traditional Asian dictator: Shuharto, Sukarno, and earlier Thai coup leaders.

Thai Hua Rubber Plc, is one of Thailand's largest rubber producers and exporters, joining in a joint venture with Laotian NCX Holding Co., to grow 200,000 rai (about 61,920 acres) of rubber trees in Vientiane, Savannakhet and Bolikhamxay provides. Its first commercial output is expected by 2012, all the output for export to China and Thailand. A second project in Krabi would produce concentrated latex to be shipped

---

78   *Ibid.*, April 30, 2006, "CPF poised to open B2 billion shrimp complex." (Charoen Pokphand Foods)
79   *Ibid.*, June 12, 2006, "Fishing for business in overseas markets."
80   *Ibid.*, March 16, 2006, "Petrochemicals, oil, gas key growth areas."
81   *Ibid.*

to China, Japan, South Korea, the United States and the European Union.[82]

Ministry of Interior and the Defense Ministry

The four southern-most provinces of Narathiwat, Pattani, Songkhla, and Yala, are essentially Muslim provinces, and they constitute a cultural boundary, not always understood by Thai, especially those from the north like the Prime Minister, Thaksin Shinawatra. They require a special subtlety, as Cora DuBois has written on this point:

> Culture, like the individual psyche, or like an iceberg, is only fractionally a part of one's conscious equipment. The last thing of which the deep sea fish would be aware is the ocean. In respect to culture, most human beings resemble all too closely the fish at the bottom of the sea. Large parts of the culturally determined behavior are so imbedded in our character that they are 'perfectly natural.' How you point, when or how you laugh and cry, what you consider edible, the proprieties of sex and procreation – these are things everyone learns as surely as he learns table manners and how to spell. The task of every person today who feels a serious sense of citizenship is to expand his cultural horizons by evaluating his own cultural heritage, at the same time that he fathoms and makes useful increasing portions of his total mind, as opposed to his logical and conscious one. The history of our generation dare not be written by the near-sighted. Our responsibilities are too great and too urgent.[83]

Distrust and suspicion of Islamic leaders in the deep South has heightened tensions in the area after the recent capture of Al Qaeda leader Hambali in Ayuthaya August 15, 2003. Anyone wearing long

---

82 *Ibid.*, August 7, 2006, "Thai Hua picks Laos, pursues Michelin deal."
83 DuBois, Cora, *Social Forces in Southeast Asia*, Cambridge: Harvard University Press, 1959. 78 pages

white shirts and with long beards is suspect. Hambali's capture in a coordinated activity is well documented as he was planning attacks in Thailand during the Asia-Pacific Economic Cooperation (Apec) summit, which would have been attended by 21 world leaders including President George W. Bush, in October 2003.[84] The United States paid $10 million for that coordinated capture.[85]

Almost simultaneously, Thailand was preparing to send Thai troops to Iraq, and Col. Boonchu Kerdchot, led the advanced team already in Iraq. The Defense Minister explained to his 447 Thai engineers and medical staff what conditions would be like. "Our forces will not be there on a combat mission but to help rebuild Iraq and provide humanitarian assistance to its people." The Thai deployment was under a mandate from the United Nations and not from the United States.[86]

Most of the Thais received a warm welcome, "They told us we were very brave because we were the first foreign troops to come to talk to them at their homes." "I told my interpreter to tell them we were there to rebuild their town and the army nurses were there to look after them. I said whatever help they needed, they should tell us." The most pressing request was to rebuild the damaged schools, and we started planning immediately.[87]

The successes of the Thai troops in Iraq, is not being translated for the Southern provinces of Thailand itself. In October 2004, the Army quelled a riot in Takbai, narathiwat province killing six and detained 1,300 people, packing them tightly on a handful of trucks, wherein 78 suffocated in transit. 84 dead in this one incident, and the Prime Minister says, "it is clear we did nothing wrong, they died because they had been fasting for Ramadan"[88] A Thai senate delegation demanded

---

84 *Washington Post*, August 15, 2003, "Al Qaeda Figure Seized in Thailand," and *Bangkok Post*, August 8, 2006, "Arrest of the 'ultimate mastermind.'"
85 *Bangkok Post*, September 18, 2003, "PM: Bounty will be parceled out fairly."
86 *Ibid.*, September 15, 2003, "Mission to Iraq."
87 *Ibid.*, October 12, 2003. "Thai door-knock wins Iraqi hearts."
88 *The Economist*, October 30, 2004, "Thaksin the callous."

the Army find the people responsible for the deaths of 78 southern Muslim detainees, and 1,290 remaining protesters were moved to less crowded quarters in three other southern cities.[89] His Majesty the King has told the government to handle the troubles "with care," and give local people a say in their problems.[90]

This is still a festering problem in 2006, as retiring Senator Fakhruddin Boto was shot in his home district of Harathiwat, and teachers are regularly under threat. Mrs. Karima Masalaeh, was arrested for instigating attacks on teachers to pressure for the release of her husband.[91]

The inability of the Defense Ministry to understand how its policies, in Southern Thailand are inflaming more violence are coming into the political dialogue leading to the elections now scheduled for October 2006. The Democrat Party leader Abhisit Vejjajiva is challenging Caretaker Prime Minister Thaksin to find more constructive measures to solve the violence in the deep Southern provinces where people are living in fear. The Minister of Defense, Gen. Thammarak Isarangura Na Ayutthaya, saying, "the authorities must learn how to hit back instead of just permitting the insurgents to hit them," and that "sweet talk alone" did no good. After the government continues to hold 1290 "rioters" in detention camps; and after the government has disbanded the National Reconciliation Commission, disagreeing with its recommendations. The dominant Thai Buddhist military and police leadership, does not understand how to deal with those across the *cultural boundary* in Muslim Southern Thailand.[92]

---

89 *Bangkok Post*, October 29, 2004, "General News."
90 *Ibid.*, November 2, 2004, "King urges restraint in South."; and May 22, 2006, "Army vows rapid rescue."
91 *Ibid.*, August 7, 2006, "Gunmen 'roam the South': Minister."
92 *Banglok Post*, August 6, 2006, "Abhisit, Thaksin clash on South policy."

Thailand Plunges in Global Ratings

In 2003 Thailand ranked 10th in global ratings for strong, and efficient government, in 2006 Thailand ranks 32rd as measured by the International Institute for Management Development (IMD).[93] The total responsibility is Thaksin's: his policies in the Southern provinces have demolished his standing among leaders in the elite leadership in Bangkok, and his policies regarding his family wealth and TRT friends gaining wealth with enhanced positions in state corporations has added to his opponents' strength as demonstrated in street rallies.

Speaking at a Rotary Club luncheon in Bangkok on August 19, 2003, Dr. Ammar Siamwalla, economist with the Thailand Development Research Institute said state-owned banks had been the main tool for the Thaksin government in financing populist programs such as the village investment funds, farm debt suspension and universal health care. He suggested very close monitoring over the next three to four years was needed to see what the final impact such policies would have on the economy. He commented that the build-up of domestic debt was a concern for the future, noting that low interest rates now hid the true costs of these programs. "if public funds were spent in areas yielding insufficient rates of return, it could potentially lead to a new economic crisis in the future."[94]

China and India Sign Treaty of Amity and Cooperation with ASEAN

China and India Sign Treaty of Amity and Cooperation with ASEAN, in Bali on October 8, 2003, becoming strategic partners for peace and prosperity. In the years since then, India's Tata Steel has bought 40% of the Bangkok-Siam Cement Plc holdings in Millennium

---

93 *IMO World Competitiveness Yearbook 2006. cf. The New Republic*, February 23, 2004, "Wrong Man."
94 *Bangkok Post*, August 20, 2003, "Populist capitalism' lifting consumption but not efficiency"

Steel Plc, and Thailand's Bangpu Plc has purchased five coal-fired power plants across China.[95]

ASEAN nations are also benefiting from Japanese investment. New investment will focus on advanced technology, research and development to support Japanese investment in the region and outside. As well, Japanese companies are growing more interested in the region's capital and financial markets and infrastructure. Mr. Kakutaro Kitashiro, chairman of the Japan Association of Corporate Executives, said, "Asean countries had developed a bond market that would attract Japanese investors to shift from New Zealand and Australia, but investment does depend upon the business environment, and that includes good governance, transparency, suppression of corruption, intellectual property rights protection, and the readiness of the financial and capital markets.[96]

Investment flows back and forth to Asia

In October 2005 the US Department of Commerce released figures showing Asians had made record new investments in the United States, Microsoft announced it will be making major investments in Asia, including hiring 1,200 new employees. "We are bullish about Asia and are excited to see Asian economies rise back to rapid growth."[97] The EU announced an agreement to make Thailand a gateway for trade and investment in the region, and Freddric Hambuaggur, EU Commission Ambassador to Thailand said, "Thailand has favorable investment atmosphere and is well equipped with facilities and utilities."[98]

---

[95] *Ibid.*, December 15, 2005, "Siam Cement sells stake in steel firm to Tata Steel," and January 19, 2006, "Coal-mining operator to branch into China.
[96] *Ibid.*, November 25, 2005, "Japanese investors shifting from China."
[97] *Ibid.*, reporting on Eduardo Rosino, Microsoft VP for Asia, *Business Times* interview, October 31, 2005.
[98] *Ibid.*, November 14, 2005, "EU views Thailand as gateway for trade and investment."

Corporate Governance/Best Listed Firms

Twelve companies have been singled out as the top performing corporate board among the 371 companies listed on the Stock Exchange of Thailand (SET), based upon the OECD Principles of Good Corporate Governance, in two categories: Exemplary practices and Distinctive practices.

Exemplary practices: Bangkok Petroleum; Kasikornbank; PTT Plc; Siam Commercial Bank; Tipco Foods (Thailand); and Tisco Bank Plc.

Distinctive practices: Bangkok Bank; Electricity Generating Plc; PTT Exploration and Production; Ratchburi Electricity; Sahaviriya Steel; and United Communication Deputy Prime Minister Somkid Jatusripitak cited these boards as "competent, hardworking boards," serving as watchdogs for the company's operations.[99]

Khunying Jada Wattanasiritham, the president of Siam Commercial Bank, was named CEO of the year at the SET Awards Ceremony. Eight companies took home awards for corporate performance: Oishi; Siam Steel International; Siam Commercial Bank; Thai Stanley Electric; Amata Corporation; PTT Exploration and Production; Precious Shipping; and Advanced Info Service.[100]

Finance and Property Restructuring

Bangkok Commercial Asset Management (BAM) plans to sign an agreement to buy non-performing assets (NPAs) from members of the Thai Bankers' Association in August 2006. Three to four banks have agreed to sell their NPAs, classified as B and C grade, with a total value of between 30 and 40 billion baht. About half of the assets are located in Greater Bangkok. The assets will be sold in 500-million-baht batches; 60% are raw land, 20% land and buildings, and the rest are factories.

Banks are also offering properties at the NPA Grand Sale, Bangkok

---

99 *Ibid.*, November 30, 2005, "Toasts raised to country's top boards."
100 *Ibid.*, July 27, 2006, "Jada named CEO of the year."

Convention Center. First time visitor Nantana Kanchanasamut, 35, was among thousands of homebuyers attending the fair. She was looking for a small townhouse for around one million baht. "I want to spend my retirement in a provincial area. So, buying a small townhouse would be easy to sell in the future."[101]

---

[101] *Ibid.*, July 14, 2006, "BAM buying bank NPAs with more offered at grand sale."

Chapter VII

The Land of Smiles is Back to Being the Land of Coups

There has been a hiatus of a little more than two years in the writing of this report on Thailand, the Test Case! On September 18th, 2006 Thailand's Army chief seized power in the 20th coup d'etat since casting aside the absolute monarchy in 1932, and acted as a new prime minister replacing caretaker premier Thaksin Shinawatra.

The military faction under Army Commander-in-Chief Sonthi Boonyaratkalin called itself the Council for Democratic Reform under the Monarchy (CDRM), immediately dissolved the cabinet and the Senate. The Constitution of 1997 was also abolished.

Former Primer minister Thaksin Shinawatra, who was in New York for the United Nations General Assembly meeting broadcast a state of emergency and sacked General Sonthi and ordered the military to respect his deputy prime minister Chitchai Wanathasin.

To recap what had preceded this coup, it is important to know that popular protests had been mounting against Thaksin. In February he had dissolved parliament and called for a snap election to regain his legtitimacy. Thailand's three main opposition parties had boycotted that April 2nd poll, which Thaksin's Thai Rak Thai Party won. The results, however, were annulled by the constitutional court in May after Thailand's much revered King Bhumibol Adulyadej said he had found the election undemocratic and urged the judiciary to act.[102] This was a peaceful coup, and the general public largely agreed with the military officers who engineered the coup for the Council for Democratic Reform (CDR), but cautioned against hanging on to power for too long.[103]

Thaksin had followed a path that other democratically elected leaders, like Chavez in Venezuela, who enhance their power at the expense of democratic institutions; Thaksin, followed that pattern, gained popular support by pushing through policies aimed at easing the plight of the poor, with inexpensive medical care, while using handouts of food and even cash to ensure votes at election time. Repeatedly candidates were found guilty of using these tactics and disqualified to hold office; making the point that it does more harm than good to live off the largess of corrupt leaders.[104] General Sonthi moved swiftly to purge top police officers and Thaksin's close aides and former classmates at the armed forces preparatory school from key posts to prevent them from mobilizing resistance.

The Council for Democratic Reform (CDR) was cautioned to use careful legal procedures in the newly created national Counter Corruption Committee in investigating ill-gotten wealth from unscrupulous politicians under the Thaksin Shinawatra administration. The experience from 1991, where the national Peace-Keeping Council (NPKC) which staged a coup to overthrow prime minister Chatchai Choonhavan, confiscated assets of the general and nine of his men, as being unusually rich; only to have the Supreme Court rule on their cases and return the assets, after unpaid taxes were charged.[105]

---

102 *Bangkok Post.Com*, September 19, 2006. *cf.*: Thailand ranked 29.2 out of 100 in 2006; compared to 50.9 in 1998, World Bank "Governance Matters, 2006.
103 *Bangkok Post.Com*, September 21, 2006.
104 *Washington Post*, "Thai Coup Highlights Struggle Over Democracy," September 24, 2006, p. A20.
105 *Bangkok Post.Com, September 25, 2006*

General Sonthi emphasized the need for a man of integrity to become the Prime Minister, and added that a military man becomes a civilian once he is retired. Royal endorsement would be sought for an interim prime minister and for an interim charter as soon as possible. Privy Councillor Gen. Surayud Chulanont emerged as the strongest candidate for interim prime minister. Even Privy Council president Gen. Prem Tinsulanonda seemed cheerful as reports grew about Gen. Surayud.

The CDR ordered in its 27th announcement that members of the executive boards of any parties dissolved for violating political party laws will be banned from casting a vote for five years once the party dissolution order takes effect. Without the right to vote, a person will automatically lose the right to take up any political position, including ministerial posts. This is clearly aimed at the Thai Rak Thai Party leadership.

Prime Minister Surauyd Chulanont immediately after being sworn in today, October 1, 2006 announced his aim was to achieve reconciliation after the divisive years under Thaksin Shinawatra: "The country's political problems and the situation in the South are both important issues that require reconciliation and understanding to be resolved."[106]

By letter faxed from London, Tuesday, October 3, 2006, Thailand's deposed premier resigned from his once powerful party after more than 200 colleagues had quit the organization in the wake of the military coup. "I have…decided to make a sacrifice by resigning from the leadership of the Thai Rak Thai party effective starting now."[107]

The coup leader General Sonthi had been put in charge of quelling the growing southern insurgency, mainly in Muslim provinces. General Sonthi, himself a Muslim had argued that it was essential to seek out an

---

106 *Ibid. October 1, 2006*; PM Surayud was army chief from 1998 to 2002, Supreme Commander 2003, and since then a member of the Privy Council that advises His Majesty the King under Thailand's constitutional monarchy.
107 *Washington Post*, "Ousted Thai Prine Minister Quits Party," October 3, 2006.

negotiate with the rebellion's leaders, reasoning that Thaksin's advisors had rejected. The insurgency in the south was caused in large measure by Thaksin's brutal and incompetent policies in the Muslim provinces.

Mr. Thaksin had many deep flaws: gross conflicts of interest between his business interests and his regulatory and law-making powers were obvious to all; far worse were his attempts to pack independent institutions with family and political colleagues; a brutal war on drug dealers (a police license for extra-judicial killings); and gross mishandling of the southern insurgency.

On October 11, 2006, Gen. Sonthi announced he had completed a new National Legislative Assembly, drawn from segments of society and government not associated with the previous government. The pattern is one that has been adopted by Thailand since as early as October 1973, following the Student-led Coup that deposed Field Marshals Praphat and Thanom. The students called upon the monarch to organize a new government and he responded using his ideas adapted from the model conceptualized by Fred Warren Riggs as early as 1959.[108]

---

108 R. W. Riggs, *The Ecology of Public Administration*, New York: Asia Publishing House, 1961.

As conceptualized by Fred Warren Riggs in *The Ecology of Public Administration*, New York: Asia Publishing House, 1961.

Thailand Transformed: 1950-2012

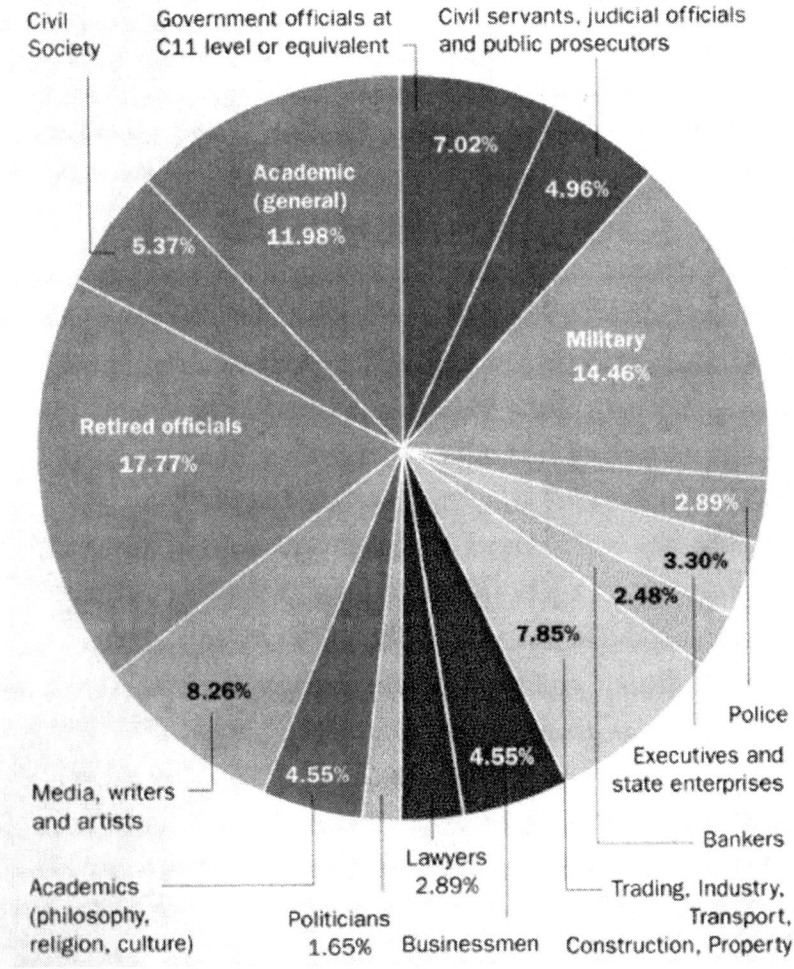

Royally inspired National Legislative Assembly.

The situation today is similar, with a group of generals seizing power. Time magazine calls His Majesty an "Asian Hero" "The King's stewardship has been so masterful that in times of crisis Thais invariably turn to one man: King Bhumibol."[109] The generals have pledged to give Thailand a fairer and lasting democratic system. Once more, the Thai people will look to King Bhumibol, trusting him to ensure that the generals keep their promise."[110]

As months passed criticism of the military junta has grown. General Sonthi addressed these issues at the end of January 2007, "The elections will happen this year." "As for the role of the army after the election, once we have a new elected government, the army will withdraw and return to their units to be a professional military." [111]

Political scientists commenting on this in Thailand clearly felt the government could be "watched over by the military" in some new ways; and business leaders were critical of the government's mismanagement of the economy, especially when they suddenly imposed capital controls meant to stem rising Thai baht values; causing the stock market to dive only to be abated after policy measures were eased.[112]

Prime Minister Surayud Chulanont has focused his concern for strengthening the police reform process, by eleciting assistance from the United Nations. The United Nations Office on Drugs and Crime (UNODC) sent in four specialists to conduct a workshop and seminar on police reform. The Police Cadet Academy opened a master's degree course for the first time since its founding in 1902. The academy joined hands with the US-based Sam Houston State University to offer the two year course in criminal justice[113] taught in English language.

By June 2006, Thailand had seen major Constitutional revisions

---

109 *Time*, November 13, 2006.
110 *Ibid*.
111 *Washington Post*, "Leader of Thai Junta Promises Vote in '07", February 1, 2007, p. A08.
112 *Ibid*.
113 *Bangkok Post*, "Specialists to draw up roadmap for reform," January 1, 2007.

and actions by the Assets Scrutiny Committee to freeze 52 billion baht belonging to premier Thaksin and family. Protests were growing seeking the ouster of the military junta. The junta's official spokesman promised that if the proposed new Constitution were defeated at the upcoming referendum they would use a revised version of the 1997 constitution, in order to allow general elections to be held on time in 2007.[114]

I was in Chiang Mai at Payap University's Crystal Spring House watching television May 24, 2007 and heard the Monarch, King Bhumibol address the judiciary en mass in Bangkok, warning that his realm was "close to sinking" and noting that "political parties must exist". One week later, the nine judges of Thailand's Constitutional Tribunal took ten hours to "outline in a marathon session, televised live on May 30th, the electoral-fraud cases against the country's two main political parties (and several small ones)." "They explained in elaborate detail why Thai Rak Thai (TRT), the largest, was being disbanded, whereas the opponent, the Democrat Party, was cleared of all charges."[115]

As one of the nine judges commented, "will apply the spirit of the coup-makers." Thus, in June it looked quite like democracy was being restricted. The Bangkok Post editorialized that "It is advisable that the people acquire some understanding of the draft charter, so they can vote for or against it in the referendum in an informed manner, rather than being led by the nose by vested-interest groups."[116] And, went on to say, "street protests are not one of the rules;" "But whether or not the banned executives are amnestied in the future, there can be no misconstruing the fact that the Thai Rak Thai party was guilty of electoral fraud, as has been indisputably proven in court."

---

114 *Ibid.*, June 10, 2007.
115 *The Economist*, June 2, 2007.
116 *Ibid.*, "Playing Politics by the Rules." June 7, 2007.

Give Dialogue a Chance

Privy Council president Prem Tinsulanonda accompanied by Commander-in-Chief of the Royal Thai Army Sonthi Boonyaratkalin led a delegation of senior officials to visit the insurgency-plagued southern region to meet local authorities as violence has been continuing. Violence in Yala, Pattani, and Narathiwat province claimed three more lives, adding to the more than 1,300 lives lost since it erupted in early 2004.[117]

During the Caretaker phase Caretaker Defense Minister Gen. Thammarak Isarangkura na Ayudhaya declined to give Gen. Sonthi policy powers in dealing with the insurgency. Caretaker Premier Thaksin Shinawatra gave the army commander "full authority" to quell the unrest. "But General Sonthi, a rare Muslim in a senior post, wanted to negotiate with the rebels, Mr. Thaksin did not."[118]

Thaksin Shinawatra, a policeman-turned-telecommunications tycoon-turned politician, followed heavy-handed tactics in quelling a new spate of violence in the three southern provinces, leading to several bloody crackdowns on Muslims in 2004. These included the Krue Sae Mosque attack on young Muslim militants and the Tak Bai atrocity, when more than 80 protestors died from suffocation when they were tied up and piled like cordwood on trucks to a detention center.

The south has been troubled for decades by separatist activities. The three province area was once an independent Islamic sultanate called Pattani. Pattani was first conquered by Bangkok in 1786 but it was not until 1902 that direct Thai rule was enforced. The Caretaker government officials have reinforced the feelings or religious and cultural alienation from the predominantly Buddhist Thai state, that has existed

---

117 *Bangkok Post*, August 14, 2006.
118 *The Economist*, October 28, 2008, p. 52. "This may have been one reason for the coup that the army chief led last month. Surayud Chulanont, a retired general and now interim prime minister, promises a softer approach to the conflict."

for decades (really centuries). More than 80 percent of the two million people in the three-province region are Muslim.[119]

On May 29. 2007 the Bangkok Post, published a story of Malaysian, Indonesian and Saudi Arabian firms signing an agreement to build the first trans-peninsula oil transmission pipeline to divert 20% of oil flowing through the Malacca Straits. It would cut through the northern Malaysian states of Kedah, Perak, and Kelantan with support at each end for deep-draught tankers. Project to begin in 2008 and operational in 2011; during the Vietnam Conflict American Army officials had proposed such a pipeline through Thailand, repeatedly the Thais had declined to build it. Now, Malaysia is building it, and the Thai provinces are missing the development they all wanted.

During the year 2007, violence continued in the south with total deaths increasing to at least 2,800. Savage mobs carried out unspeakable crimes against random individuals with the claim that the perpetrators have suffered so greatly that any act is justified. At no time have the insurgents issued a call for justice. Rather, they have used claims of such crimes to justify their outrageous and indefensible attacks on teachers and innocent victims. "At some point, true community leaders must encourage people to denounce extremism and barbaric murders, and communities must respond."[120] Local residents from all walks of life must help watch the community.

Economic Development under Coup Leadership

In January 2006, Mr. Thaksin had briefed 1,300 foreign investors about the mega-projects Thailand was contemplating under its modernization framework . They were projects in the areas of transport, water management, information networks, defense, agriculture, science and technology, culture and public health. All these projects

---

119 *Bangkok Post*, October 5, 2006.
120 *Ibid.*, "The necessity of moderation," December 4, 2007.

were suspended after PM. Thaksin dissolved the parliament. Now in September following the Coup d'etat the Thailand Development Research Institute (TDRI) urges the new government to revise the entire structure of those plans to ensure their economic feasibility and value.[121]

Forward thinking economists saw the need to revise economic strategies to focus on stainable growth and improving the well-being of the Thai people. Realistically, they saw Thailand being challenged in the world's markets by China, India, and an emerging Vietnam. Productivity must be increased and a search should be initiated for another growth engine as a substitute for the United States. Sectors like tourism, retirement homes, medical care, and animation should be considered. The "sufficiency philosophy" may be the most suitable framework for Thailand's future development.[122]

Five electric train lines with a combined length of 118 kilometers and an estimated cost of 165 billion baht received official backing from the government, with construction set to be completed within six years. These projects are now changed from purely state enterprises, as under the Thaksin government, to joint state-private enterprises. Wherein the state will bear the costs of civil engineering work, designs, and land expropriation, while the private sector will be invited to invest in trains and signal systems. Prime Minister Surayud would like to sound out public opinion on the environmental impacts of the railway lines and the suitability of the proposed routes.[123]

The Energy ministry announced it was scrapping a measure which guaranteed 50% of all new electricity production capacity to the Electricity Generating Authority of Thailand (EGAT). Egat must now

---

121 *Bangkok Post*, September 26, 2006
122 *Ibid.*, "State advised to focus on sustainable growth," October 30, 2006.
123 *Ibid.*, "Five electric train routes win backing," November 8, 2006; Siam Cement Plc's $225-million petrochemical project in Iran is back on track after a delay caused by conflict over Teheran's nuclear program.

participate in bidding for new independent power projects if it wants to build new power plants. Either Egat or private producers who offer the lowest power rates would be the successful bidders.[124] This action reveals how Mr. Thaksin and others conspired to control the bidding process for a costly software project vitiating the EGAT reputation for transparent and open process. The Democrat Party demanded an investigation.[125] It was in the push to privatize Egat that Mr. Thaksin was caught up scheming with others in an illegitimate process, and the beginning of the end of his government.[126]

Power Adjustments

The spontaneous protests in separate provinces over planned power projects reflects the need for public participation in the national energy policies. More than 45, 000 names have been submitted in Samut Songkhram province opposed to construction of coal-fired power plants. Locals speak of having heard of the adverse consequences of existing coal-fired power plants in Mae Moh district and in the industrial estates in Rayong.

Clean natural gas is used to produce 70% of the electricity by total fuel volume, coal is used for 15% of current generation. Those ratios need to change, and the Energy Policy and Planning Office suggests two options, 50:50 ratio of gas to coal and the other would be 70% natural gas to 30 % coal. Cost-wise, clean coal is certainly a consideration that Thailand needs to weigh; however, the national Energy Policy Council has set up a committee to study the possibility of building a nuclear power plant in Thailand.[127]

---

124 *Ibid.*, "State utility must bid for new IPPs," November 9, 2006.
125 *Ibid.*, "Democrats demand Egat graft probe," December 10, 2006.
126 *Ibid.*, "Egat Case Brought Privatisation to a Halt," December 29, 2006.
127 *Ibid.*, Nuclear power plant panel to be set up," March 2, 2007; *cf.*, "Thailand to 'go nuclear' by 2020, June 11, 2007.

Thailand Ranks 5ᵗʰ in Foreign Capital Inflows

After China, Hong Kong, Singapore and India according to the recent United nations Conference on Trade and Development (UNCTAD) report. Thailand received $9.8 billion in 2006. A survey of the American Chambers of Commerce (Amcham) members indicated 75% thought the Coup and subsequent policies like the 30% reserve requirement were major factors for future investment in Thailand; with just 40% thinking of expanding operations here.[128]

The Democrat Party leader Abhisit Vejjajiva, suggests the 30% reserve rule should be scrapped, to revive investor confidence and increase foreign inflows. This is rebutted by the Bank of Thailand (BoT) which imposed the 30% rule to thwart speculation on the Thai currency, the baht. Mrs. Pongpen, BoT Senior Director, has recently said foreign direct investment (FDI) was still flowing into Thailand normally, and the 30% foreign capital reserve requirement had not measurably eroded foreign investor's confidence.[129]

Thailand's International Contracting

The Thai Petrochemical Industries (TPI) now controlled by PPTPlc., is known as IRPC with a ten year old refinery which produces 120 liters per year of high sulphur petrol currently banned in Thailand, where more than half the population live in urban areas, has entered into a sales agreement with Southern Yunnan Province China for export there. Shipments are by way of the Mekong River from Chiang Rai province to Xishuangbanna Gas and Petroleum.[130]

Researched by IIR, Kosit Panpeimras, Minister of Industry, and DOW Chemical officials, agreed to seek DOW Board approval for five petrochemical projects in Thailand, valued at $1 billion to $2 billion.[131]

---

128 *Ibid.*, "US Chamber Calls for 'Positive steps." March 20, 2007.
129 *Ibid.*, "Central Bank Opposes Lifting 30 pct Reserve," February 9, 2008.
130 *Bangkok Post Newspaper*, "High-Sulphur petrol a windfall for IRPC", May 29, 2007, p. B1.
131 *Washington Post*, June 19, 2007.

Thailand's economy has been driven by strong exports this year, which surged more than 18 per cent during the first six months, but has started to slow in July, These observations were by the Fitch Ratings (Thailand) representative, James McCormack, addressing a conference on the Thai economy's prospects, "relative to the investing bank's own equity capital" was at Bank Thai with 21 per cent of its own equity, followed by the Bank of China with 17 per cent.[132]

Japanese are very food conscious and food safety is important as Chinese practices are revealed as compromised, Japanese food processors have relocated from China back to Thailand. The National Food Institute (NFI) said exports of food products this year (2007) are expected to reach $17.72 billion, up 18.3% from last year. In baht terms exports are projected at 608.04 billion baht, up 7.8% from last year. NFI said food exports in 2008 are expected to rise at least 10% in both US dollar and baht terms.[133]

Proposed Expansion of Chinese-Thai Traditional Trade

Few western economists realize that Bangkok is not the largest port of entry for Chinese products into Thailand. Chiang Saen port in Chiang Rai province on the Mekong River is the largest port of entry in tonnage annually. Due to the Chinese construction of three large dams on the upper reaches of the Mekong River in China water flows are much restricted in the lower states of Thailand, Laos, Cambodia and Vietnam. The Chinese are now proposing to blast rocks in stretches of the Mekong and then to dredge a channel to allow 200-ton cargo vessels to navigate the river to restore trade now restricted by low water levels.[134]

Villagers living along the Mekong River are convinced that poor

---

132 *Bangkok Post*, "Pour fragile economy," September 3, 2007.
133 *Ibid.*, "Food Hygiene and Safety Scares," October 11, 2007; *cf.*, "China milk scandal 'can help Thai exports, "October 9, 2008.
134 *Bangkok Post*, "China unveils plans for blasting Mekong river reefs," 12/21/2006

management of the Chinese Dams is causing the flooding in the lower Mekong. It was very different from previous experience with Mekong River flows. The water rose very quickly and the current was stronger than usual. We want to know when they open or close the dams and how they affect the lower Mekong. Sometimes the rising water is simply inconsistent with rainfall volume.[135]

Thailand and China Open Linkage Discussions

Largely due to the reduced Mekong River flows, China and Thailand are now discussing road and rail linkages so that cargo may flow freely between their states. Two bridges exist across the Mekong now: Nong Khai-Vietiane and the Mukdahan-Savannakhet bridges. Significant development follows each such construction and now a third bridge at Chiang Khong district of Chiang Rai province will link across the Mekong to Ban Huay Sai of Bo Kaew province in Laos. Funding will be jointly by Chinese and Thai governments.[136]

A Thai-Korean joint venture company is developing a large area for a five-star hotel and a golf course in Ban Huay Sai; while a Chinese consortium is planning to build a 30,000 rai industrial estate in Tung Sam Mon in Chiang Khong district as a center for processed agricultural products and other export goods for China. On the Laos side a 500 km road known as R3A is being built to Chiang Rung in southern China.[137]

On May 29, 2007 the Bangkok Post announced that Prime Minister Surayud had met with both President Hu Jintao and Premier Wen Jiabao in Beijing to sign a joint action plan for strategic cooperation including the building of a railway line to link Yunnan province with Chiang Khong in Chiang Rai province, Thailand.

---

135 *Ibid.*, "Chinese dams still blamed for floods." August 21, 2008.
136 *Bangkok Post*, "New Thai-Laos bridge throws up old problems," April 22, 2007.
137 *Ibid.*

Thailand as an Export Driven Economy

The modern Thai economy has expanded vastly upon its historic export trade patterns. The Mekong River was a major trade and transit route over the centuries. Agricultural goods constituted the major flows of goods between Thailand and China. In 1971 while studying Thai language in Bangkok, I was one of several students invited by Father Lim, a Chinese catholic priest to join him for a luncheon where he ordered a special fruit dish from his home province in China. It is standard to have shipments world-wide of such fruits and other delicacies for meals in Chinese restaurants. And Thai rice has a special connotation worldwide in Asian markets and restaurants.

Beginning in 1974, General Motors entered Thailand for automotive and pick-up truck manufacturing not to eliminate others but to join in the marketing of products demanded across south Asia. In 2007, Thailand is the home of 15 auto manufacturers with a combined production of 1.5 million passenger cars and 2.8 million motorcycles annually. Importantly, there are more than 2,000 auto parts producers in the country. Thailand's auto exports now account for half the country's total production of one million cars; while promoting energy-saving cars as another champion product after the one-ton pick-up trucks. Vehicles for export totaled 330,296 units or 52.7% of total vehicle production.[138]

Thailand's economy is projected to grow this year by 4.5% revised upward from the earlier estimated 3.8-4.3%, with a stronger performance of 4.5 to 5.5% expected in 2008. At present exports comprise almost 60 per cent of the Thai economy.[139]

Cross-Border Agreements are a Key for Growth

The need to negotiate with Laotian government officials to adjust policies at border checkpoints has become dramatically important as

---

138 *Bangkok Post*, "Production expands 2.5%, led by exports," September 24, 2007.
139 *Ibid.*, "Exports continue to drive Thai economy," November 27, 2007.

Highway 9 has been expanded from the Mukdahan bridge through Laos to Danang in Vietnam and the South China Sea. Similarly, as the road network from Chiang Khong in Chiang Rai province to Jing Hong, Yunnan province China has been completed, a 1,400 kilometer passage through Laos.[140] The result of this Greater Mekong Subregion (GMS) negotiation is the promotion of bilateral logistics investments: for distribution centers, warehouses, and truck terminals. Geographically, Thailand perceives itself as the logistics hub of the region. The Thai kingdom is in the middle of southeast asia, and its laem Chabang deep seaport, which handled 4.3 million containers in 2006, can expect to see an increase to 6.2 million containers over the next two years.[141]

The Chinese Defense minister General Cao Gangchuan held talks with Prime Minister Gen. Surayud Chulaniont as a follow-up on the earlier talks with the Chinese President Hu Jintao and Premier Wen Jiabao, December 3, 2007 in Bangkok. They discussed the need for military cooperation, including training and technology transfer, together with the suggested connection of roads and railways from Thailand to Yunnan and Guangzi through Laos and Vietnam. The Defense Minister said he would discuss nuclear technology transfer to Thailand to build a nuclear power plant with respective agencies in China; and he pledged full cooperation to Thailand.[142]

Iran Holds out Possibility of Gas Pipeline

Davoud Danesh Jafari, Iran's Finance minister speaking in India raised the political stakes in Southeast Asia, at least another notch by suggesting that the planned Iran-Pakistan-India pipeline could be extended to Thailand. "We are very positive about the (Iran-Pakistan-India) pipeline 3, 2008. Because we firmly believe that it will have a

---

140 *Ibid.*, "Transport Trade Logistics," September 25, 2007.
141 *Ibid.*
142 *Bangkok Post*, "China to consider Thai-proposed nuclear energy," December 3, 2007.

regional impact." "We are positive we can take the pipeline to Southeast Asia, to countries like Thailand, Malaysia, and Singapore."[143]

Complicating the deep relationships between Iran and Thailand are petrochemical project investments by Thai firms in Iranian developments. National Petrochemical Pcl, which is 38% owned by state petroleum giant PTT, and Cementhai Chemical Co. Ltd. (CCC), a wholly owned subsidiary of Siam Cement. The problem arises from the World Bank insuring the two giant Thai firms, with development loans for projects in Laos.[144]

Industry/Steel and Investment

China's Baosteel Group Corp., is planning to build a smelter in Thailand to meet rising demand. Global steel firms have been drawn to Thailand by strong domestic demand, which has grown in line with sectors that use steel as a raw material, including automotives, electrical appliances, and electronics, and canned food. Thailand consumes between 12.5 million and 13 million tons of steel per year. Demand for steel products may rise to 25 million tons per year over the next decade, and Thai company's still produce only low-quality products, while high-grade steel products are mostly imported from Japan and South Korea.[145]

Following on the announcement of a steel smelter for high-grade steel in Thailand, General Motors announced plans in August 2008 to invest $445 million to build a new plant to manufacture clean, green turbo-diesel engines in Thailand. Then, following the financial crisis of September, GM announced a delay.[146]

---

143 Ibid., "Iran holds out possibility of gas pipeline," Jan. 20, 2008. *Note:* "In recent years, Iran has tried to split the Thai-US relationship with high-level diplomacy and sweet deals on oil and rice trades."
144 Ibid., "Next Big Scandal?" February 2, 2008.
145 Ibid., "China's Baosteel pitches smelter," February 3, 2008.
146 Ibid., "GM delays Thai diesel project," November 28, 2008.

TAGS Wins Mideast Contracts

Thai Airport Ground Services is planning to expand heavily in the Middle East after the company recently secured contracts to provide airport services in Iraq and Sudan. TAGS, was founded in 1990 by the Airports Authority of Thailand offers services including cargo and passenger handling, technical aircraft and line maintenance. Customers include Unite Airlines, Northwest Airlines, Qantas, Lufthans, Japan Airlines, UPS, DHL, and FedEx. "Our target is simple – to be the best total solutions provider for the aviation industry in Asia[147]

The Changed Tide of Traditional River Know-How

In the years before the 1960s flooding was common place along Thailand's rivers. As they flooded the people waded up to their knees in Bangkok, and other cities along rivers, it was simply to be expected seasonally. Changes began in the late 1960s and during the decade of the 1970s. The arrival of Linne Tholin, retired Chief Engineer of Chicago, Illinois, brought highest quality technical expertise to bear on water flow and wastewater treatment problems. Chicago at the base of Lake Michigan with heavy snow melt and rain storms meant moving water out and down the Illinois River. Bangkok did not have snow melt problems, but it does have monsoon storms and flooding as an historic fact.

As a consultant to the Lord Mayor of Bangkok, Linne tackled these problems head-on. The installation of a drainage system for central Bangkok to pump surface water out into the Chao Phraya River, transformed life in the city as long as the pumps were turned on. It did in fact take the king's intervention to keep them turned on and pumping. And, by 2006, the Governor of Bangkok, Apirak Kosayodhin "vows no Bangkok floods," "because 17 new water gates will be opened this week."[148]

---

147 *Ibid.*, "Iraq, Sudan deals to build 'airport cities'" December 10, 2008.
148 *Bangkok Post*, September 24, 2006.

A whole new attitude has emerged where a water pump controller can now be hailed as a "community savior" and 33-year old Amnat Gekhuntod is a man with a mission, especially when it is raining cats and dogs. His job is to keep floodwater at bay in the Prawet district of Bangkok. Mr. Amnat says he is proud to be a flood fighter who is always busy dredging canals, draining excess water and removing rubbish from drainage pipes. "I feel good when my neighbors come to thank me and give me moral support. Some bring food and energy drinks to cheer me up."[149]

Heavy rains in northern Thailand were threatening to overflow the Bhumibol Dam in Tak, and the Royal Irrigation Department Chief, Samart Chokkanapitak said he was confident the network of dams: Bhumibol, Pasak Cholasit and the Sirikit Dams now existing would restrain the flood waters.[150] A month later, a large percentage, nearly three-fourth of those asked said they were happy with the solutions to the flooding that the government did accomplish.[151]

But a year later, headlines read, "Governor vows no major Bangkok floods," and water quality is now a major issue following the Queen's birthday address stating her concerns for the public to conserve the waters of the Chao Phraya River, and Governor Apirak launched a project to treat wastewater in 80 canals connected to the Chao Phraya.

Bangkok Metropolitan Administration (BMA) has seven wastewater treatment facilities, and needs three more at Bang Sue, Klongtoey and Thomburi to treat 992,000 cubic meters of wastewater. He added however, that there are 16,365 factories registered in Bangkok and a number of them have not yet installed wastewater treatment systems, and they should do so before their water is expelled into the Chao Phraya River.[152] Clearly, Thailand is wrestlying with basic sanitation issues that perplex much of Asia today as they modernize and develop industries.

---

149 *Ibid.*, "Man on a Mission," October 8, 2006.
150 *Ibid.*, "Bhumibol dam nears capacity," October 9, 3006.
151 *Ibid.*, "Bangkok appreciates lack of flooding," November 2, 2006.
152 *Ibid.*, "More treatment units for Chao Phraya," August 15, 2007.

Ancient Law of King Mangrai

This 700 year old law from the Lanna Dynasty detailed the code of water management. The election of a Kair Fai was a similar process to voting in a board meeting. Representatives of villagers would convene in a meeting held in a forest at night. The village people could remove a Kair Fai from a position if they found their leader to be incompetent or unscrupulous. The law gave the Kair Fai the power to block waterways, divert waters and allocate waters. They used weir dams to control water flows. Por Mouen supervises Phya Kum weir (dyke), which is one of 12 ancient weirs built across the Ping River, a major lifeblood in the northern region. Now, the Royal irrigation Department (RID) is changing entire policies by building floodgates, dams and removing ancient weirs.[153]

Tsunami Created Awareness

The December 24, 2004 Tsunami killed 5,000 people and injured 11,000 more. Now 100 towers are being built along the 800-kilo-meter coastline. Tests to alert the citizens were not successful because public relations were not effective. They must do better in the future! Similarly towers are being built in other regions to alert people to floods and air pollution. Measurements in the provinces of Chiang Rai and Mae Hong Son of dust-particulate levels were at health-threatening levels: dust and particulate matter were measured at 148 and 212 micrograms per cubic meter in the two provinces respectively.[154] The maximum health standard of 120 micrograms per cubic meter is being far exceeded.[155] This air pollution is a regional problem that needs a regional solution: Yunnan province, China, Burma, Laos, and Thailand all need to work on this problem.

---

153 *Ibid.*, "Villagers in northern provinces are divided in their opinions concerning the newly proposed water scheme by the city," December 4, 2008.
154 *Ibid.*, April 8, 2007.
155 *Ibid.*, "Stop this practice of burn-offs," March 15, 2007.

Chapter VIII

Basic Education Policies

Thailand has been undergoing massive changes in education over the fifty years studied in this report. Initially, fourth grade education was rather the nation-wide standard, yet by 2006, the nation's policies looked toward funding 12-year basic education fully subsidized.[156] The higher rates were seen as unavoidable in that it was the only way to truly offer a good basic education in state-run schools at all levels, from kindergarten to high school, as required under the national Education Act.

Rectors of 24 state universities pleaded their cause for privatization and further for a reinstatement of the University Affairs Ministry to handle higher education administration.[157] It was the Rectors feeling that the Ministry of Education simply does not pay much attention to the human resources development at higher education institutions. It was the earlier policy under the University Affairs Ministry to seek royal endorsement on academic titles for lecturers directly, now all academic titles must first win approval of the Ministry of Education, purely a bureaucratic and time consuming policy.

Under the Coup government of Prime Minister Surayud Chulanont

---

156 *Bangkok Post*, "Higher school subsidies likely to get green light," October 23, 2006.
157 *Ibid.*, "Rectors call for end to red tape," October 15, 2006.

the National Legislative Assembly (NLA), the appointed Upper House of the Parliament, continues to debate policy. Among the issues debated are: effective tax collection, with the suggestion that local administrative organization be allowed to increase local taxes and to improve local tax collections;[158] Privatization of public universities, with an attendant shift of tuition to the individual students and a reduced cost on governmental budgets. Needless to say that suggestion of new tuition costs caused student protests.[159] At least 200 to 300 students were to demonstrate their opposition to the bill to free Thailand's most prestigious universities from the state. The NLA unanimously supported the draft bills allowing King Mongkut's Institute of Technology, Chulalongkorn, and Thaksin universities to leave the bureaucratic system.

Islam in State Schools

In a measure to restore peace in the majority-Muslim South, Prime Minister Surayud Chulanont has proposed religious instruction at all public schools in the Muslim South. Thailand's Bangkok-based, predominantly Buddhist central government has restricted Islamic studies and the Yawi language instruction at public schools in the past, deeming it more important that the local population learn to be "Thai" and speak the language. The Foreign Ministry was assigned the responsibility to coordinate with the Malaysian government and study what educational syllabus is needed to be improved for primary education.[160] This coup government has taken a much more conciliatory approach to the conflict than his predecessor, but even so, violence has escalated.

---

158 *Ibid.*, "Local tax collection flaws," Suggested by NLA Member Ammar Siamwalla, November 24, 2006.
159 *Ibid.*, "Chula students to rally against autonomy," December 8, 2006.
160 *Ibid.*, Prime Minister backs Islam in state schools," January 27, 2007.

Thailand's IT Potential

Thai students put the county on the technology map following their success in the Imagine Cup competition held in Seoul, South Korea. This global competition staged by Microsoft is seen as the world's premier competition for technology students. 3KC Returns team was the overall winner of the Software Design Invitational, they beat more than 100,000 students from over 100 countries and were awarded a $25,000 cash prize for their efforts. The theme of this year's competition was "Imagine a world where technology enables a better education for all." The 3KC Returns team focused on "literacy" as the solution to achieve such a goal. "This inspired us to create a software program to help children and illiterate people to read and enjoy the books that they would like to read."[161]

Nurses Training for Southern Provinces

The newly appointed government of Prime Minister Samak Sundaravej met with the visiting Prime Minister Shaikh Khalifa bin Salman Al Khalifa of Bahrain, to initiate a Thai government training program for 3,000 nurses, mostly natives of the three troubled southern provinces. Once trained these nurses would be sent to work in hospitals of Bahrain. Bahrain has had representatives working in those three provinces to assist the Thai government in assessing the causes of violence in the southern provinces. This agreement is an outgrowth of that work.[162]

Universities Hit by "Brain Drain"

Faculty enjoy full lifelong pensions after working for 10 years at state universities, and as a result some universities are finding long-serving staff are resigning to receive better salaries in the private sector, while retaining their lifelong pension rights. Public universities have been

---

161 *Ibid.*, "A Win for Thailand," August 29, 2007.
162 *Ibid.*, "Thailand to train 3,000 nurses for Bahrain," February 9, 2008.

encouraged to take state-affiliated status by the Education ministry to give them more freedom in financial and resource management, with only a limited regulation by the state; however, the change was unexpectedly stimulating good lecturers and staff to leave.[163] The country has 78 state and 68 public universities, reported by the Higher Education Commission, an agency under the Ministry of Education. The problem has become acute in the fields of public health, medicine, and nursing in the past 10 months, private operators are poaching staff.

---

163 *Ibid.*, December 10, 2008.

Chapter IX

Constitution Drafting

It must be noted that even after a Thai Coup D'Etat a legislative body continues to exist. That body is the National legislative Assembly (NLA) which is an appointed upper house of the Legislature of Thailand. This was created beginning in 1973 after the student-led Revolution. If you were to compare it to the British system it is the House of Lords; it really is an inspired creation of the King of Thailand, who adopted and adapted the Prismatic Concepts of Fred Warren Riggs.[164]

On October 10, 2006, the Chairman of the military Council for National Security (CNS) and Royal Thai Army commander-in-chief General Sonthi Boonyaratkalin announced the selection of 250 members of the NLA as a new body to draft a new constitution, which would be convened as soon as royal endorsement had been obtained.

Gen. Sonthi said that the assembly members were drawn from professional groups and various sectors of the society to work to complete the document before the next election scheduled for next October 2007, when sovereignty will be returned to the Thai people.

So who is Coup'ed? It is the lower house, the elected house of Representatives, their elected prime Minister and his Cabinet! The

---

164 See Supra, Ch. VII, Page 99.

coup of September 19, 2006 removed the elected members of Thailand's government replacing it with a military Council for National Security (CNS).

The Constitution of 1997 allowed Thaksin Shinawatra to take authority into his hands and commit acts the generals saw as monopolizing power and the political environment to the detriment of Thailand. The CNS prefers to see possible Prime Ministers from outside the elected legislature, term limitations, prevention of mergers of political parties after an election, and the prohibition of caretaker governments after new elections are called, wherein the civil service would run the county during election periods. The problem which faces the general is that the highly participatory 1997 Constitution has given the voting public a taste of participatory democratic rule that cannot be deleted from its collective consciousness, and is a bench-mark by which to judge future charters.[165] Without question, the Thai military does not trust politicians.

The CNS announced that a Constitution Drafting Assembly (CDA) would consist of 100 members and their elected President was former Thammasat University rector, Noranit Sethabutr, with first and second deputy chairmen, former Senator Seri Suwannapanont and former lawmaker and charter writer Decho Sawananont. His Majesty the King Bhumibol Adulyadej endorsed these appointments.[166]

The Constitution Drafting Assembly (CDA) approved the creation of a 35-member constitution drafting committee (CDC) after it received a list of 10 drafter from the Council for National Security; 25 Members are from the CDA and 10 members are from the CNS. The CNS urged that Sqn-Ldr Prasong Soonsiri, a member of the NLA be appointed chairman of the drafting panel because he had ability to cope with criticism. It is likely that the panel will be bombarded with criticism

---

165 *Bangkok Post*, "Analysis: Military's constitutional goals will split society," December 22, 2006.
166 *Ibid.*, January 11, 2007.

during the next six month as the charter is being written, "Only a person with strong mental strength can survive [heavy criticism]. A person with cold feet may bow out [of the post] easily.[167]

And immediately, the issue of a special status for religion is raised by devout members of society, and though it has been cast aside the 1997 People's Constitution has set an enlightened path for Thailand. It's Section 38: "A person shall enjoy full liberty to profess a religion, a religious sect or creed, and observe religious precepts or exercise a form of worship in accordance with his or her belief, provided it is not contrary to his or her civic duties, public order or good morals."

"In exercising the liberty referred to in paragraph one, a person is protected from any act of the State which is derogatory to his or her rights or detrimental to his or her due benefits on the grounds of professing a religion, a religious sect or creed or observing religious precepts or exercising a form of worship in accordance with his or her different belief from that of others."[168]

By April 1, 2007, members of the Election commission (EC) were predicting the general election would be held in December. Both Commissioners Sodsri Sattayatham and Prephan Naiyakovit were expressing that feeling based on the PM's comment that the Constitution Drafting Committee would be complete with a draft no later than July 6 thus allowing for a referendum before September 2, 2007. The CDC told the CDA that their panel had held 537 forums and surveyed the opinions of 36,324 individuals throughout Thailand. The majority wanted the Prime Minister to be an elected MP (68.2%), that senators be elected (67.9%); and an end to subsidies for political parties. (71%). Half the people thought parliamentarians should have at least a bachelor's degree, while 40.9% wanted the number of MPs reduced to 400.

---

167 *Bangkok Post*, "A test of wills on constitution writing," January 24, 2007.
168 *Ibid.*, "Editorial: Religion needs no special status," February 16, 2007.

The results of a poll taken among the constitution writers themselves showed the majority preferred that the prime minister be chosen from the ranks of the elected MPs (75%); that the number of MPs and senators be reduced (63.1%) and that parliamentarians have at least a bachelor's degree (66.1%). Strong support was expressed for scrapping the party-list system (46.2%) and that senators be appointed, not elected (41.5%).[169]

The Constitution Drafting Committee (CDC) decided five key issues, including the prime ministership, the size of the House of Representatives, and the make-up of the Senate. The main thrust was the requirement that a prime minister come from the election process. The panel of drafters also agreed at their meeting to reduce the number of MPs from 500 to 400. The House will consist of 320 constituency MPs and 80 party-list MPs. They also agreed the senators should be appointed, not elected. These five key issues were the most controversial in the process of writing the constitution. In an additional two weeks the panel will present its constitution to the full Constitution Drafting Assembly (CDA) for concurrence by all 100 members.[170]

After weeks of fine-tuning, the CDC decided to select the 80 proportional representatives from eight groups of provinces, with each political party offering a list of 10 candidates for each provincial grouping. For the Senate, the CDC resolved there will be 150 senators, 76 of them elected directly, one from each province. The remaining 74 senators will be selected from the professions. After three years in office, half of the 74 professional senators will have to leave the chamber. A lot-drawing process will decide who exits the Senate.[171] It was specified that women must be candidates in each election category without a fixed quota.

---

169 *Ibid.*, April 2, 2007.
170 *Ibid.*, April 10, 2007.
171 *Bangkok Post*, "CDC settles on system of representation," June 8, 2007.

Constitution Drafting Assembly Accepts the Draft

It was announced on July 6th, that the Constitution Drafting Assembly (CDA) had voted unanimously to accept the draft constitution, 98-0 with two members absent. The CDA Chairman, Noranit Setabutr suggested dates for publicizing the constitution on July 31st, with the provisional referendum scheduled for August 19th. Once the draft constitution was accepted and the election was held, Sqn-ldr Prasong Soonsiri added the military would return to their barracks.[172]

During the next month leading to the referendum pro and cons were discussed and finally it was editorialized: "Ignore the propagandist rhetoric and let your conscience be your guide. Vote with your conscience on what you feel will best benefit the country, bearing in mind that the country, which has been mired in political uncertainty for almost two years, needs to free itself from military rule or the semblance of it, and to move forward towards parliamentary democracy."[173]

Referendum Endorses Thailand's 18th Constitution

Thailand's first-ever referendum has endorsed the country's 18th constitution that promises to weaken the political party system and strengthen the hand of the bureaucracy and military, final results showed with 57.41 per cent voting yes, 42.19 per cent no and the remainder were invalid. Some 25.9 million out of 45.6 million eligible voters, or about 57.6 per cent participated in the referendum. The military is satisfied with the people's acceptance, said General Sonthi Boonyaratkalin, who led the junta that ousted Thaksin. Political analysts said the results show a deeply divided Thailand.[174]

"This vote shows that the polarization of Thailand is entrenched…

---

172 *Ibid.*, "Constitution gets unanimous approval," July 6, 2007.
173 *Ibid.*, "Editorial: History is in the making," August 18, 2007.
174 *Ibid.*, "Thailand's Referendum Endorses Army-Backed Charter," August 20, 2007.

It signifies a deeply divided country."¹⁷⁵ Political turmoil had begun in January 2006, when a strong anti-Thaksin movement took off in Bangkok with open-air speeches criticizing Thaksin and his government.

The general election of 2001 was won by Thaksin Shinawatra, a former telecommunications tycoon whose populist platform used slick campaigning gimmicks that won him the backing of rural poor and the disgruntled urban poor and middle classes. His good delivery on those campaign promises won his Thai Rak Thai (Thais Love Thais) Party an overwhelming majority in the 2005 election, giving Thaksin an unprecedented parliamentary majority that allowed him to run over his opposition and independent bodies established by the 1997 Constitution to provide checks and balances to executive power. Those abuses of power led directly to his eventual downfall at the hands of the military in the September 19, 2006 coup d'etat.

While the 1997 constitution was written to strengthen the political parties against their traditional downfalls, weak and corrupt coalition governments that led to military coups, the 2007 draft constitution essentially strengthens the hand of the bureaucracy, including the military, at the expense of the political parties. A strength of the 2007 draft is its increase of the people's participation in politics, while a weakness is article 309 which grants amnesty for coup makers and legitimizes the military's future role as an overseer of Thai politics.[176]

Democrat Party leader Abhisit Vejjajiva interviewed by Channel 3 television expressed his concern: "As the votes for and against the draft charter are so close, it means amendments to the charter are necessary." And, Thai Rak Thai group member Surapong Suebwonglee concurred stressing the need for cooperation in order to lift the country out of the current political stalemate.[177] Even the Bangkok Post editorialized "A

---

175 *Ibid.*, Dr. Thitinan Pongsudhirak, director the Thailand's Institute of Security and International Studies.
176 *Ibid.*
177 *Bangkok Post*, "Abhisit: Charter needs to be fixed." August 20, 2007.

Need for good Governance" yet no coalescence occurred and the nation moved on to the December 23rd Election.[178]

The northern and northeast regions rallied with the remnants of the now-defunct Thai Rak Thai (TRT) Party to create the People's Power Party (PPP) and elect a near majority in the legislature and named Samak Sundaravej prime minister. A village leader from the northeast, Mr. Sompong Wiangchan was prescient when he commented, "History has told us that what is written in the constitution is meaningless if it is not translated into real benefits for the people at large."[179] And others commented," The CNS and the pro-Thaksin camp must come to terms with reality and find a peaceful way out, …(or) the country will disintegrate if they continue to fight to the death."

---

178 *Ibid.*, August 23, 2007.
179 *Ibid.*, "The Race is On," August 28, 2007.

Chapter X

Thailand's Political Drama

Early in 2008, Freedom House, a US-based political monitoring group cited Thailand as being painted yellow, and that is a good thing, because all the nations around them except for Malaysia are dark purple.

Yellow signifies "partly free," while the foreboding darkness means they are not free at all! Dark purple signifies lacking in both a decent democratic system and proper human rights protections. The yellow color is a promotion for the post-coup Thailand. It signifies that the country has now adopted a constitution and a parliament that came from a free election.

The road ahead for Thailand is neither clear nor certain. Democracy is a messy form of government, subject to abuses from many sides and fictions. As statesmen have often cited, it is the worst system, except for all the others.

In February 2008, it could be said that,"PM Samak Sundaravej's past history in national and local administration includes a troubling tendency towards the autocratic and arrogant method of making decisions. That will no longer do. Voters will demand explanations… they have a right to ask and government has the duty to answer."[180]

---

180 *Bangkok Post*, "Editorial: Worst system, bar the rest," February 2, 2008.

A steady purging of government officials and cabinet members continued through the summer of 2008 as the Democrat Party led the cleaning process. The on-going struggle between the People's Power Party (ex-TRT) and the People's Alliance for Democracy (PAD) is revealed in the efforts to rewrite the constitution versus efforts to force the government to hold back for a time.[181]

By October 2008, the situation has changed dramatically, and the anti-government People's Alliance for Democracy (PAD) led by Sondhi Limthongkul and Maj-Gen Chamlong Srimuang are rallying large demonstrations at the parliament building. Direct confrontations of anti-riot police and PAD demonstrators are becoming more violent.[182]

The current Prime Minister is Somchai Wangsawat, brother-in-law of Thaksin Shinawatra, who is trying to compromise with the PAD and yet allow the parliament to proceed with its business. Even with the violence, the army refuses to take the bait offered to coup d'etat the government merely saying it is politics and should be settled politically.[183]

"More than 400 people were injured in the clashes, including at least six protesters who had limbs blown off, news agencies reported. Police say they used only tear gas canisters, but some protesters dispute that in view of the severity of some of the injuries. About 20 police were also reported injured, several of them with gunshot wounds, news agencies said." "Charging that the police used excessive force, several hundred doctors and nurses dressed in black marched on the national police headquarters Thursday and demanded that the government step down."[184]

"With the political system in deadlock, many Thais are looking to the country's revered monarch, King Bhumibol Adulyadej, to use

---

181 *Ibid.*, July 14, 2008.
182 *Ibid.*, August 27, and October 7, 2008.
183 *Washington Post*, "Thailand's Political Drama Spirals Into Violence, Financial Crisis," Oct.9, 2008.
184 *Ibid.*

his moral authority to save Thailand from itself. But given that the stalemate has descended to a zero-sum game-what would satisfy one side would automatically alienate the other- it is difficult to see how even he could find a satisfactory way out of this impasse."[185]

PAD Mass Protests Special Coverage

Bangkok Post Associate Editor Sanitsuda Ekachai, makes the very important point, "One of the things the Oct. 7 crackdown shows is that we have a much more open society." And she goes on to remind us that the legendary newsman Sanpasit Viriyasiri tried to broadcast the October 6, 1976 storming of Thammasart University by the police and military, and he was immediately fired.[186] But, she concludes her commentary saying, "If we see the authoritarian culture as our biggest stumbling block to democracy, the place to begin is in our heart. Democracy cannot exist where there is no basic respect for human rights and dignity."[187]

October and November 2008 saw continual confrontations of PAD yellow-shirts and UDD (United Front of Democracy against Dictatorship) red-shirts, inspite of efforts at reconciliation. And, PAD denies the legitimacy of the government as a Thaksin puppet.[188]

PAD Wrong to Block Airport

The PAD's reason for the road blockage – to prevent Prime Minster Somchai Wongsawat from returning home from Peru, where he had been attending the APEC summit. The resulting traffic jams blocked everyone and resulted in extreme inconvenience for all the people who need to use the airport. "This latest action by the People's Alliance for Democracy comes closer to terrorizing the public."[189]

---

185 *Ibid.*
186 *Bangkok Post*, Commentary, October 9, 2008.
187 *Ibid.*
188 *Bangkok Post*, Editorial: Time for rest from protests, November 24, 2008.
189 *Bangkok Post*, editorial, November 25, 2008.

PAD leaders now committed to close the airports for the next five days and stranding 350,000 travellers in Thailand. Special flights were arranged by Spain, England, Russia, and the Philippienes, departing form U-Tapao, Chiang Mai, and Phuket. Interim Prime Minister Somchai Wongsawat landed in Chiang Mai and governed from there. "The PAD, clad in yellow, have vowed to keep Thailand cut off from the world until Mr. Somchai the brother-in-law of the hated ex-premier Thaksin Shinawatra, steps down."[190]

In rapid fire fashion, Thai Airways has declared it will sue PAD for the airport blockages, and the Constitutional Court has dissolved the PPP for election fraud. This puts the government out of office and the bargaining begins to form a new government. And the Army is actively discussing ways to form a new government.[191]

"The opposition Democrat Party announced it had mustered the backing of 260 lawmakers in the 400-seat lower house, allowing it to form a government with Oxford-educated party leader Abhisit Vejjajiva as the new prime minister."[192]

---

190 *Washington Post*, "Government Backers Rally in Bangkok," December 1, 2008. NOTE: "Many of the senior officers in the security forces are drawn from the same class of elites that form the core leadership of the PAD and share many of the same aims. Somchai and Thaksin have drawn their support primarily from the rural poor."
191 *Bangkok Post*, "Newin 'key to new govt'" December 4, 2008.
192 *Washington Post*, "Thai opposition says it can form next government," December 6, 2008.

Chapter XI

Thailand's Rocky Road Ahead

Airlines seek redress for PAD actions

IATA the International Air Transport Association, which represents 230 airlines accounting for 93% of scheduled international air traffic worldwide, has suggested that the Thai government follow the precedent set by the United States government which compensated airlines and others in the travel industry after the 9/11 terrorist attacks. IATA has offered to work with the Airports of Thailand (AoT) to identify costs and make sure they are not passed on to the airlines, while declining to get involved in the internal politics of Thailand.[193]

AoT reported passenger traffic through Suvarnabhumi fell to an average of 55,737 a day, down from about 100,000 in the pre-seizure period. Flights dropped from 714 daily to 496, while cargo declined from 3,365 tons to 2,395 tons. IATA has recommended that the Thai state-controlled airport company waive landing and parking fees for airlines for six to 12 months, just to get them back to Thai airports.[194]

---

193 *Bangkok Post*, "Concern about AoT passing on costs," December 14, 2008.
194 *Ibid*.

We need a PM we can trust

Monday, December 15, 2008, Thailand got its third prime minister in four months, after Democrat leader, Abhisit Vejjajiva was voted into power ending six months of political paralysis. The vote was called after Somchai Wongsawat was removed from office 10 days ago by the country's constitutional court, which found his party guilty of irregularities in elections held last December 2007.[195] Vejjajiva, a British-born economist, won a parliamentary vote against former national police chief Pracha Promnok.

Vejjajiva, 44, has promised a rapid disbursement of government funds to try and revive the economy, but with tourism, exports, and foreign direct investment all reeling from the double blow of global economic slowdown and the recent domestic turmoil, this government faces substantial challenges.[196] Finally having fulfilled his dream of becoming the Prime Minister, and receiving Royal Endorsement, Mr. Abhisit will now have to prove he is a capable leader. "He will have to prove his party is more trustworthy and has a higher capability to steer the country out of the crisis than its political rival which has fallen from power for committing electoral fraud."[197]

Prime Minister Abhisit is quoted by the Alliance Francois Press (AFP) that protesters who occupied government offices and blockaded the two Bangkok Airports should be held legally accountable for their actions.[198] The PAD campaign culminated in an eight-day blockade of Bangkok's airports late November that left about 350,000 travellers stranded.

Thailand's prime minister unveiled his new Cabinet, including a supporter of the airport blockade, casting doubt upon the ability of

---

195 *Washington Post*, "Former Opposition Leader Chosen as Thailand's PM," December 15, 2008.
196 *Ibid.*, *Cf.*, *Bangkok Post*, "A Grand Plan," December 17, 2008.
197 *Bangkok Post*, Editorial, December 19, 2008.
198 *Bangkok Post*, "Abhisit says PAD must face the music," December 19, 2008.

this government to unite the divided nation. Foreign Minister Kasit Piromya, 64, a career diplomat who hailed the airport blockades as "new innovations for public protests," is unlikely to help heal the rifts, and was cited as a "necessary compromise" to keep the coalition factions satisfied! Finance minister is Korn Chatikavanij, an Oxford-classmate of the PM, a respected economist and former investment banker, who headed JP Morgan Chase & Co.in Thailand from 1999-2004; and, Interior Minister Chavarat Charnvirakul, 72, a former Thaksin supporter who switched sides to join the Democrats.[199]

Thai Premier leans Right to Placate Bargain Factors That Put Him in Power

"It is the military's dividend for putting Abhisit in power."[200] Violations of human rights of Burmese refugees is the issue which is alleged that Thai military towed hundreds of Rohingya ethnic minority refugees out to sea rather than allowing them to land in Thailand. Abhisit has stated, "The military has maintained that it has not breached any humanitarian principles on this issue."

Abhisit has also come under criticism for his administration's enthusiastic support for the country's draconian "lese majeste" laws, which are intended to protect the dignity of the royal family but which his critics say are being used to muzzle political debate and intimidate opponents.[201] In view of these criticisms, Professor Thitinan Pongsudhirak says, "the supposed clean government and the rule of law policies are finding a gap between rhetoric and reality, and it seems to be growing wider."

---

199 *Washington Post*, "Thailand's new government endorsed by the king," December 20, 2008.
200 *Washington Post*, "New Thai Premier Seen as Leaning Right," January 30, 2009.
201 *Ibid.*, Several prominent people have been charged under the law which carries a mandatory jail sentence of 3 to 15 years for those found guilty.

Rough Economic and Political Challenges

As the world economy has tumbled Thailand has discovered it too must use Keynesian deficit-funded stimulus packages to cause things to return to normal, or at least break the fall. "In the long term, Asians have to consume more, and Europe and the U.S. have to consume less."[202]

The deposed former prime minister Thaksin Shinawatra makes phone-in rallies to his Untied Front for Democracy against Dictatorship (UDD) followers (red-shirts) urging them to get the Puea Thai Party leaders organized for an amnesty, so he can safely return to lead the country again.[203] Former TRT leader Chavarat Charnvirakul now Interior Minister forced the hands of the Democrats by telling a gathering of local administrators their salaries would be doubled this year, to thunderous applause. The Democrats' Finance Minister Korn Chatikavanij was not amused. But they had to go along, and agreed to do it in two phases, one half this year and the second half next year.[204] Puea Thai Party forced a no confidence vote, and Prime Minister Abhisit Vejjajiva easily survived.[205]

Pro-Thaksin Rallies Grow

Rallies were held in more than 10 provinces on Monday, March 30, 2009. The intention of these red-shirted rallies is clear. "But the government will not fall into this trap. We will be patient."[206] The red-shirt protesters rallied at provincial halls, with some camping out for the night. The demonstrators in Bangkok remained at their site outside Government House. Broadcasts of the Bangkok rally were relayed to

---

202 *Washington Post*, "S.E. Asia Faces Long-Term Trade shift," February 7, 2009.
203 *Bangkok Post*, "All-Party talks on amnesty bill urged," February 14, 2009.
204 *Bangkok Post*, "The Democrats' 'marriage' is heading for the rocks," March 15, 2009.
205 *Washington Post*, "Thai PM, ministers easily survive censure vote," March 21, 2009.
206 *Bangkok Post*, Suthep Thangsuban, Deputy Prime Minister. March 31, 2009.

provincial protesters. "We will keep fighting until we get democracy back," Thaksin said in a video broadcast from an unknown location to the rallies last night.[207]

The Dawning of New Realities

Traditional Thai politics, had an unspoken rule, that if you were ousted from power, you just stayed low, kept your bitterness to yourself, let the dust settle, and you would soon be allowed to return home to enjoy the riches you had accumulated, minus the political power you once had.[208] "The fugitive former prime minister has refused to play by the old rules, choosing instead to stir up a storm to reclaim power and-if that fails- to bring his enemies down with him…His giant ego and fierce stubbornness definitely play a role in his political tantrums."[209]

From a sleepy, rice-growing agrarian society, with a set of beliefs to maintain working relations in a highly hierarchical and unequal society, the rush to modernize the country during these past four decades has opened up society and given the populace new aspirations which challenge the old norms. A new feeling is present in our society as to what you can and cannot do, people naturally embrace any new criteria that make them feel more free or more equal. Each group is seeking their own different answers, while democracy is being differently defined.

Like it or not, Thaksin's refusal to play by the old political rules and the support he gets from the red shirts are also indicative of Thailand's new realities. The fundamental issue for Thailand then is: How to preserve peace among competing interests while fostering an open environment that is more equal and free?[210]

---

207 *Ibid.*
208 *Bangkok Post*, Commentary, by Sanitsuda Ekachai, April 1, 2009.
209 *Ibid.*
210 *Ibid.*

Conclusions on the Thai Developmental Model for Asia

Thai commitment to United Nations requests, funding assistance and responsible leadership in world affairs has produced a unique model for development. This Buddhist nation's willingness to accept others ideas and permit free idea exchange has indeed contributed to its steady development. Thailand in the midst of Southeast Asia poses the possibility that its success may inspire some neighboring nations to try change themselves, as we now see occurring in China. If this is *soft power*, and I am sure it is; it stands in sharp contrast to the violence now seen in the Middle East, where the United States leadership has embroiled us.

The keys to the Thai developmental model begin with education and training, Fulbright Act assistance, technical assistance and then with defense assistance. The subtleties of World Bank assistance, coupled with the side-by-side training of engineers to carry out their scientific tasks with bureaucratic integrity. The three decades of the 1950s, 1960s and the 1970s spelled increased education and training for a responsible bureaucracy, and we see that value as Thais carry on even in times of political turmoil.

The steady hand of the Thai monarch over 60 years has produced growth, unity of peoples, and pride in being a Thai. The current weaknesses we see in the political leadership, are having significant effects, and the opponents are rallying to act as a democratic check, and the legal system under the Thai Constitution is acting to remedy corruption of the leader and his party.[211]

King Bhumibol Adulyadej, the American-born third child, of Prince Mahidol has quietly led the nation for 60 years in the developmental process, recently cited by the United Nations as the "Development King" in an award by Secretary General Kofi Annan, May 27, 2006; and cited by the US Congress in a Joint Resolution No. 409, on the occasion

---

211 *Bangkok Post*, July 26, 2006, "Second Bid for Freedom thrown out."

of the 60th anniversary of His Majesty's accession to the throne.[212] The People's Republic of China President Hu Jintao sent a message of blessing to the Thai monarch on this occasion of his 60th anniversary of accession to the throne.[213]

The 60th Ceremony included ancient ceremonies dating back to the Sukhothai era in the 13th century. The King lit candles and incense in homage to the Buddha. With the Crown Prince, he presented holy offerings to the monks. Ninety-nine monks recited blessings for His Majesty in Pali, the ancient language of the Buddha. In a second rite, the Chief Court Brahmin presented lustral water and sacred leaves to their Majesties. Since ancient times in India the leaves have been believed to eliminate evil influences at a King's coronation. His Majesty then poured holy water over the Royal insignia and Regalia. From ancient times the six items of the regalia have represented the King as

Ruler and have brought unity to the people. They symbolize kingly power, justice, peace, and the duty of the king to ensure the welfare of all his subjects.[214]

King Bhumibol is the longest reigning monarch in the world and his 60th Ceremony was attended by the world's royalty. Some pictures are included herewith.

---

212 *Ibid.*, May 26, 2006, "Kofi Annan honours 'Development King,'" and June 23, 2006, "US Congress honors King."
213 *Ibid.*, June 1, 2006, "China congratulates HM the King."
214 *Ibid.*, June 10, 2006, "King conducts ancient ceremony."

Thailand Transformed: 1950-2012

By Permission: Bureau of the Royal Household,
The Grand Palace, Bangkok, Thailand.

RAMA IX, King Bhumibol Adulyadej and Queen Sirikit greeting European Royals on the Occasion of His 60th Anniversary Celebration of Monarchy in 2006.

Chapter XII

THAILAND: An On-Going Struggle for Democracy

Thailand's Supreme Court Confiscates B46.37bn from Thaksin

Ousted premier Thaksin Shinawatra speaking to his red-shirt Puea Thai Party supporters from the United Arab Emirates saying it was an "unfair" decision. He began by apologizing to his family. "He said his ex-wife Khunging Potjaman na Pombejra had told him long ago that they had enough money and that he did not need to get involved in politics."[215]

The majority of judges decided to seize 6.8 billion baht in dividends and 39 billion baht from the sale of Shin Corp. shares, totaling B46.37 bn. "The dividends and the sale of the shares in Shin Corp. is wealth acquired through inappropriate means," the judges said.[216] The Court allowed Thaksin to keep Bt30.72bn.

Finance Minister Korn Chatikavanij has commented on this case as follows: "I became involved with the assets concealment issue when Thaksin sold his shareholdings in Shin Corp to Temasek Holdings of

---

215 *Bangkok Post*, "Thaksin to cope with 'unfair' verdict." February 26, 2010.
216 *Ibid.*

Singapore in January 2006, a year after I became an opposition Member of Parliament. I remember that all of Thaksin's actions at that time indicated that he was the real owner of the assets and had hidden all of his shareholdings all along." "Thaksin flew to Singapore to negotiate the sale of Shin Corp shares while informing the public that he was on a leisure trip. He hurriedly amended the legislation on shareholding limits under the Telecom Act so that he could sell his shareholdings and he did everything he could in order to avoid paying tax."[217]

At that time I did two things: First, I pointed out that there was evidence at the Securities and Exchange Commission (SEC) indicating that Thaksin secretly owned his Shin Corp shares via an account at Singapore UBS Bank. Second, I filed a complaint with the Revenue Department that the transactions involving the transfer of shared to Thaksin's children carried a tax liability."[218]

It is out of this background that Thaksin has consistently acted to keep his followers stirred up and moving toward open rebellion. The majority of his followers are from the North and Northeast regions of Thailand and represent rural communities that feel an affinity for him, a non-royalist politician.

The Leaders of PAD and UDD

It is possible now in retrospect to name the leaders of these two movements who have been stirring Thai politics for the past decade. The People's Alliance for Democracy (PAD) ahs been led by Maj. Gen. Chamlong Srimuang, Sondhi Limthongkul, Pibhop Dhongchai, somsak Kosaisuk, Somkiat Pongpaiboon, Suriyasai Katasila, Chaiwat Sinsuwong, Amorn Amornratananont, and Therdphum Jaidee.

The United Front of Democracy against Dictatorship (UDD) has

---

217 *Bangkok Post*, "Personal reflections in the Assets seizure case," March 5, 2010.
218 *Ibid*. On May 3, 2010, The Comptroller General's Department reported B49bn assets transferred from six commercial banks to the state.

been led by Veera Musikhapong, Natthawut Saikua, Jatuporn Prompan, together with maj. Gen. Khattiya Sawasdipol (known as Sseh Daeng), Weng Tojirakam, Kwanchai Praipana, Wiputhalaeng pattanaphumthai, Yotwawaris Chulom alias Jeng Dokchik, Korkaew Pikulthong and Nisit Sinthuprai.[219]

The violent clashes in Bangkok from March 26 to May 19, 2010 were led by UDD leaders and focused the attention of the Thai Government on issues raised by the Red-Shirted men, women and children from rural Thailand as had never occurred before.[220] Calls for the Army to lead a Coup were rejected by the Army Chief Anupong Paochinda as he had done since 2007, when he declared, "…he was a classmate of former prime minister Thaksin Shinawatra in Class 10 of the pre-cadet school, but he will not allow this personal matter to mix with his duties and responsibilities for the country."[221] This is a rarely heard comment placing country above personal loyalty commitments among classmates as Thaksin rallied his colleague police officers to himself.

Beginning on Friday, March 19, 2010, a crimson tide of protesters snaked its way through the 40 miles of street of Bangkok meeting often sympathetic crowds revealing a level of support in the capital quite unexpected by the Thai press. "I haven't seen any opposition from Bangkok people. People were thankful. They came to cheer us from all walks of life. They gave water and food to us…They all want democracy back." Jatuporn Prompan, said "their art work will be the history of the people's fight for democracy."[222]

Veera Musikhapong announced at the Phan Fa Bridge rally Friday March 26, 2010 that the UDD protesters would meet Sunday at the 11th Infantry Regiment at 9 am and "we hope to meet the prime minister

---

219 *Bangkok Post*, June 16 and July 18, 2010.
220 *Bangkok Post*, "The Red Crisis" Interactive Graphic by Choopong Eamoraphan, July 1, 2010.
221 *Bangkok Post*, "Anupong: 'No new coup'" November 3, 2007.
222 *Bangkok Post*, "Thai protesters' caravan wends through capital," March 20, 2010.

there, and if not, he should step down. We hope tomorrow will be the end of the political problems."[223]

Prime Minister Abhisit has held firmly that he will not step down giving in to Red Shirt pressures even while the Election Commission (EC) reviews challenges to the Democrat Party. "For the past month, the demonstrators have occupied a symbolic swathe of Bangkok's old city, in a campaign to force an early election against the wishes of Mr. Abhisit, whose term ends next year. The protests have been peaceful, but the capital has been shaken by a string of unsolved bombings. Protesters also seized a second site in a posh shopping area and on April 7th briefly invaded parliament, giving Mr. Abhisit a pretext to declare a state of emergency in and around Bangkok."[224]

In the afternoon of Saturday, April 10th, the Army advanced along the tree lined streets toward the red shirts' encampment and an exchange occurred, lasting an hour. Black-clad men armed with assault rifles and explosives appeared to participate. It has become apparent that this protest has moved beyond a simple Thaksin support movement to one revealing a split within the army itself. There is a name for those who are moving toward the red shirts: "watermelons" i.e., green outside, red inside.[225]

Academics Urge Political Talks

Surichai Wankaew of Chulalongkorn University said both sides should return to talk, but his time the talks must be made in a closed door. The peace talk is needed to prevent violent clash between the people and soldiers. Law Faculty Dean at Thammasat University Somkid Lertphaithoon said UDD should vacate Ratchaprasong intersection and move in front of Government House instead.[226]

---

223 *Bangkok Post*, UDD to see PM at regiment Sunday. March 27, 2010.
224 *The Economist*, "Martyrs on both sides," April 17th, 2010, page 45.
225 *Ibid.*, at 46.
226 *Bangkok Post*, "Academics urge political talks," April 24, 2010.

Use of force still an option for the army[227]

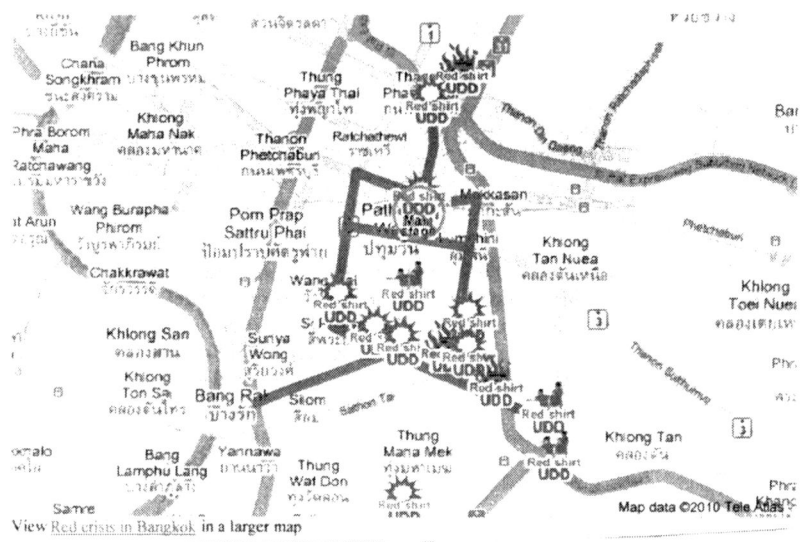

[1] Ibid., Earlier Story., May 19, 2010.
[2] Bangkok Post, Statement by Acting Government spokesman Panitan Wattanayagorn, May 21, 2010.
[3] Bangkok Post, "Thai PM, saying violence quelled, calls for unity," May 21, 2010.

PM meets with governors in red rallies

Prime Minister Abhisit Vejjajiva met with governors of 61 provinces Sunday, asking them to build understanding among local residents that the protest at Ratchaprasong is against the law and asked them to take a legal action against local media broadcasting distorted information.[228]

Not the same Silom anymore

Thursday night, April 22, an explosion in the Silom/Sala Daeng area shook buildings and began a confrontation of red-shirt protesters and the Army. Skywalks are barricaded and many shops are closed. "At our office, there is a plan to allow employees to work at home. They also want us to stay neutral and stay away from the crowd and (any

---

227 *Bangkok Post*, Army spokesman Sansern Kaewkamnerd said if the situation goes beyond gov't control.
228 *Bangkok Post*, "PM meets with governors on red rallies," April 25, 2010.

confrontation) for our own safety, said Mr. Nicha Kwandee, a 28-year old office worker in Silom.[229]

Red shirts get 15 days in jail

The Thanyaburi Court on Tuesday sentenced 11 leaders of the red shirts who blocked Phayon Yothin highway on Monday, April 26th, evening and checked citybound vehicles to prevent police and soldiers from entering Bangkok, to 15 days each in jail without suspension. UDD attorneys are offering 50,000 Baht for each defendants bail. The bail request is being considered by the Court.[230]

PAD renews call for swift end to protests

As Maj Gen. Chamlong and Mr. Pibhop hand letters to both government spokesmen and army Maj gen. Jiradet Sitpranete calling for the army to take action. Thai troops are confronting protesters who were rallying at the Talad Thai wholesale market when the seasonal downpour dispersed the crowd.[231]

New Thai violence kills 2, mars compromise moves

On May 8th, Prime Minister Abhisit Vejjajiva has stepped up to put an end to the political crisis in Bangkok by agreeing to a House dissolution in September and a General Election to be held November 14th, 2010. The coalition partners agree; the private sector applauds; the academics nod their approval; and the international community supports the compromise. Even the red-shirt UDD has accepted the prime minister's road map toward reconciliation. But the date for withdrawal from Ratchaprasong and other sites is not yet agreed.[232] "Hopes for an

---

229 *Bangkok Post*, "Residents and vendors count the cost of Thursday's violence, April 25, 2010.
230 *Bangkok Post*, April 27, 2010.
231 *The Washington Post*, Tim Johnson reports, Thai troops clash with protestors, April 29, 2010; *Bangkok Post*, April 29, 2010.
232 *Bangkok Post*, "Beware of the reds – and keep your eyes on the yellows" May 9, 2010.

end to Thailand's political crisis diminished Saturday following a new eruption of violence that killed two policemen and wounded 13 people in double night-time attacks."[233]

The prime minister wouldn't have offered the November 14 compromise if he wasn't confident that the Democrat Party can win the general election in six months. After all, weeks of shuffling, transferring, and appointing the right people both civil and Police in bureaucracies of the north and northeast have made it better for the Democrat Party. That is the way politics goes.[234]

'Guilty' Seh Daeng faces dismissal, stripping of rank

Pro-red shirt Maj. Gen. Khattiya Sawasdipol, widely known as Seh Daeng, faces the prospect of being sacked from the army after a Defense Ministry panel found him guilty in "military criminal cases." "What have I done wrong? I've protected the army chief from being verbally attacked by the yellow shirts and now I am protecting the lives of innocent people (red shirt protesters)," he said.[235]

---

233 *The Washington Post*, Denis D. Gray reports, "The official Erawan Emergency Center said two policemen were killed in the two incidents, and the wounded were believed to be police."
234 *Bangkok Post*, Commentary by Editor Voranai Vanijaka, May 9, 2010.
235 *Bangkok Post*, Reported by Wassana Nanuam, May 8, 2010.

Thailand Transformed: 1950-2012

[1] Bangkok Post, Commentary by Editor Voranai Vanijaka, May 9, 2010.
[2] Bangkok Post, Reported by Wassana Nanuam, May 8, 2010.

Thailand sizzles as temperatures go through the roof

Ranging from Bangkok at 103 to Phrae and Tak over 108 (43 C), with health officials fearing there will be heat stroke and deaths due to the high temperatures.[236]

PM Abhisit offered to hold new elections on November 14, but the Red Shirts then set a series of conditions that proved too much for the prime minister. He rescinded his offer and ordered the security operation. "The government's containment operation got off to a bloody start Thursday evening. Maj. Gen. Khattija Sawasdipol[237],a renegade army officer whom the prime minister once described as the greatest obstacle to peace, was shot in the head, the apparent victim of a sniper's bullet. He dies four days later.

The volatility of the situation forced the United States and Britain to close their embassies near the protest zone Friday. Several other embassies, including those of Japan, New Zealand, and the Netherlands also closed. At least three journalists were among those wounded. Nelson Rand, a Canadian cameraman working for a French television channel, was shot on the abdomen and hand.[238]

Pathumwan district court handed down six-month jail terms to 27 red-shirts who were arrested from Friday's clashes between protesters and troops. They violated the emergency decree enforced in the capital by engaging in political gatherings of more than five people. To the families of people at the protest: tell them that the rally is illegal and the court will hand down heavy sentences without probation.[239]

---

236 *Bangkok Post*, Heat Trap: Maximum Temperatures, May 20, 2010.
237 *The Washington Post*, "Thai troops, protesters clash in streets; wounded general remains in coma," May 14, 2010.
238 *Ibid*.
239 *Bangkok Post*, Mr. Tharit Pengdit, Chief of the Department of Special Investigations, May 15, 2010.

Put an end to this rebellion

"Let me repeat. We reap what we sow. It's a rebellion. Put an end to it, swift, severe, and certain. Or step down and let the rebels take over. The longer this crisis drags on the closer we are and the deeper we will be in a state of anarchy."[240] "The need for the government to stand up to the red shirt mob is unarguable. But Mr. Abhisit and other ministers should make it clear they hope to end this deadly confrontation before it worsens. The red shirts need to step back, end their two-month sit-in and return Bangkok to its citizens. The government must encourage them to do so."[241]

Ultimatum passes as battles rage on in Bangkok

According to government figures, 66 people have died and more than 1,600 have been wounded since the Red Shirts began their protests in March. The toll included 37 killed, almost all of them civilians, and 266 wounded since Thursday.[242]

Government rules out talks unless rally ends

The Center for the Resolution of the Emergency Situation (CRES) announced in a televised statement on Tuesday, talks will only be held after UDD ends its protest rally.[243]

Violence erupts after red-shirt leaders surrender

Red-shirt leader Jatuporn Prompan announced from the stage at 1:15 pm that he and other leaders would surrender to prevent further losses. "I apologize to you all but I don't want any more losses. I am devastated too. We will surrender." He also announced the ending of the anti-government protest.[244]

---

240 *Bangkok Post*, Article by Editor Voranai Vanijaka, May 16, 2010.
241 *Bangkok Post*, Editorial, "Never too late for peace talks," May 17, 2010.
242 *The Washington Post*, Reported by Denis D. Gray, May 17, 2010.
243 *Bangkok Post*, "Gov't: Talks only after rally ends." May 8, 2010.
244 *Bangkok Post*, Violence erupts after red-shirt leaders surrender. May 19, 2010.

The announcement did not put an end to waves of rioting and arsoning around the capital. Many key buildings were set ablaze such as up-market Central World shopping complex near the Ratchaprasong intersection, the TV Channel 3 station, a section of the Stock Exchange of Thailand (SET) building and the Metropolitan Electricity Authority Office were set ablaze. CRES imposed a curfew in Bangkok from 8 pm to 6 am. Thais and foreign residents were asked to stay home.[245] The rioters set fire to 27 buildings around Bangkok during the day.

Troops retake area around main protest site

Troops reclaimed part of the area around the Ratchaprasong intersection rally site on Wednesday morning, using armoured personnel carriers to destroy barricades of tyres and bamboo set up by the protesters as clashes between troops and protesters continued around the capital. "Protesters wishing to return home can board buses at the National Stadium," said government spokesman Panitan Wattanayakorn[246] At least four people, including an Italian reporter, were killed and more than 50 were wounded in the operation, local media reported.

Ousted premier Thaksin Shinawatra called on the government to hold

---

245 *Ibid.*
246 *Bangkok Post*, Troops retake area around main protest site. May 19, 2010.

direct talks with UDD leaders, saying that arranging such negotiations were way beyond him at this time. The Reds were campaigning for elections to replace the administration of Prime Minister Abhisit Vejjajiva, which they considered illegitimate because it came to power with the backing of the army in a 2008 parliamentary vote. The Reds are mostly supporters of fugitive ex-premier Thaksin Shinawatra who was ousted in a 2006 coup. A controversial court ruling ejected his elected allies from power, paving the way for Abhisit's election as prime minister by the parliament at the head of a coalition government.[247]

New task force to return city to normal

The Centre for the Resolution of the Emergency Situation (CRES) announces a special task force to ensure security for the people of Bangkok in the wake of Wednesday's political violence, and a centre to assist and rehabilitate businesses affected by the unrest.[248] Three divisions of troops scoured the area of Ratchaprasong, and will examine ten high-rise buildings by 3 pm and the area will then be returned to Bangkok Metropolitan Authority by 6 pm today. Claiming order has been restored after a spasm of violence, Thailand's prime minister made an emotional appeal to the nation to heal the political wounds that divide it. "We will continue to move swiftly to restore normalcy and we recognize that as we move ahead there are huge challenges. Let me reassure you that the government will meet those challenges."[249]

---

247 *Ibid.*, Earlier Story, May 29, 2010.
248 *Bangkok Post*, Statement by Acting Government spokesman Panitan Wattanayagorn, May 21, 2010.
249 *Bangkok Post*, "Thai PM, saying violence quelled, calls for unity," May 21, 2010.

View Red crisis in Bangkok in a larger map

[1] Ibid., Earlier Story., May 19, 2010.
[2] Bangkok Post, Statement by Acting Government spokesman Panitan Wattanayagorn. May 21, 2010.
[3] Bangkok Post, "Thai PM, saying violence quelled, calls for unity," May 21, 2010.

Unsung heroes of Klong Toey repel red threat

What happened on Na Ranong Road near the Bangkok Post office on Wednesday showed that security guards and ordinary people were able to play a role in protecting their neighbors from the violent threats if the more radical red shirts. Tossaporn said, "Villagers were on high alert." They acted to protect Loxley, Shell Thailand, Post Publishing and local residences in mainly run-down communities. "We were always sending a message to them that (the protest) had ended. Please band together to protect the community."[250]

In devastated Bangkok, residents join city workers in cleanup efforts

Maliga Agsombon, owner of a yoga health club, with two friends, answered the call from Bangkok's municipal authorities for volunteers to join city workers in a festive cleaning. She swept up garbage along

---

250 *Bangkok Post*, Unsung Heroes of Klong Toey repel red threat. May 22, 2010.

a wide boulevard near the still-smoldering carcass of a mall that used to promote itself as Thailand's 'premier lifestyle shopping destination." Nearby, workers from Starbucks – open for the first time in weeks – served iced tea to camouflage-clad Thai soldiers.[251]

Governors and Police Chiefs in NE provinces removed

Governors and Police Chiefs of Khon Kaen, Udon Thani, Mukdaharn, and Ubon Ratchathani were transferred to inactive posts or temporary duty at their respective Headquarters in Bangkok for failing to protect their city halls from fire attacks by red shirts despite order to see that all state property would be well protected.[252]

Safety concerns hang over city's 'new beginning'

Bangkok has gone from chaos to calm, but experts warn residents must now make security precautions a part of everyday life. MR (Mom Ratchawong) Sukumbhand admits City Hall faces limitations in coordinating with other agencies and with its fire-fighting capabilities. Everyone is warned that in the event of a serious crisis, residents should have cash on hand as well as adequate medical and food supplies. "The approach we'll take (on reconciliation) must be people-centered because the people of Bangkok have been deeply affected."[253] Thai Reinsurance, the country's leading reinsurer, is preparing to launch a repackaged terrorism insurance policy for local businesses. "Political riots and widespread torching have also led foreign reinsurers to think twice about quoting (premiums), as such events have never happened before in Bangkok.[254]

---

251 *The Washington Post*, Reported by Andrew Higgins, Monday, May 24, 2010. Page A-10.
252 *Bangkok Post*, Police chiefs in NE provines removed. May 27, 2010.
253 *Bangkok Post*, Article on Safety Concerns, May 29, 2010.
254 *Bangkok Post*, Thai Re will offer flexibility and value. May 31, 2010.

DSI seeks 20 new warrants for terrorism

The Department of Special Investigations is seeking warrants to arrest 20 more people on terrorism charges, including Puea Thai Party MP Karun Hosakul and red shirt leader Korkaew Pikulthong. Among those for whom warrants have already been issused are Puea Thai Party MP Jatuporn Prompan and ousted prime minister Thaksin Shinawatra. They are wanted on terrorism charges in connection with the May 19 rioting and arson attacks.[255]

> As the bullets flew and the bodies fell, crocodile tears came from afar, as Mr. Thaksin tweeted his sorrow to his followers. From his luxurious exile he denied, once again, that he was giving orders to the red-shirt leaders and urged everyone to embrace peace. There is little doubt, however, that Mr. Thaksin holds sway over the splintered, squabbling red-shirt leadership. The two-month protest would not have been possible without his deep pockets, vengeful will and political network, even though the red-shirt cause has become much larger than him. And his stubbornness seems to have undone the peace talks, despite his protestations.[256]

Thailand's Reform Efforts

PM plans to wait until dust settles

The prime minister stressed that an election should be called only when the situation had returned to normal and the political campaign and the poll must be free and fair. Some groups are still talking about fighting on and resuming a mass rally in June. Despite his saying the country was heading back to normal, the curfew was still being enforced in Bangkok and 23 provinces today from 11 pm to 4 am.[257]

---

255 *Bangkok Post*, Approval will increase list of suspects to 39. May 31, 2010.
256 *The Economist*, "A polity imploding," May 22, 2010. Page 25.
257 *Bangkok Post*, Election date depends in return to normal. May 23, 2010.

Chuan urges police reform

Former prime minister Chuan Leekpai and the Democrat party advisory chairman criticized the Thai police as ineffectual and the people did not trust the police, while the military was praised for being mature and this was the main reason that no coup happened even under the extreme crisis. In the eyes of the general public, the Thai police were ineffectual in comparison with the military. "Of course, there are some good people in the police It is the chance for the government to reform the police, but must clearly explain this to the public, must tell the truth as it will be good in the long term."[258]

Abhisit & Co. survive but parliament takes a drubbing

The two-day censure debate was contentious and ferocious at times, mediocre and tedious at others. The opposition took the opportunity to whitewash itself and former prime minister Thaksin Shinawatra from the serious charge of terrorism which the government has leveled at the red shirt leadership. The government also used the forum to defend itself against the allegation that it violently cracked down on the protesters. This is only a blame game that went on in parliament, with no side really interested in providing more information or establishing any semblance of truth- be they about the arsonists who went on a rampage around town, or the six deaths at Wat Pathumwanaram (located behind Central World in Ratchaprasong).[259]

Abhisit: Corruption root of problems

Corruption directly contributed to today's public discontent with the social, economic and political imbalances within the country. Public corruption resulted in added waste and the procurement and delivery

---

[258] *Bangkok Post*, Chuan urges police reform. May 25, 2010.
[259] *Bangkok Post*, Power Games. June 2, 2010.

of goods and services ill-matched for the country's needs at the expense of the taxpayer.[260]

Police reform panel chief appointed

Police General Vasit Dejkunchorn, was appointed chairman of the police reform committee, and charged to recruit members to improve police efficiency, image and morale.[261]

Conclusions on the Struggle for Democracy

Democracy as Abraham Lincoln would have defined it was *government of the people, by the people and for the people.* So as we look to Asia and particularly to Thailand in this paper, how are they succeeding in achieving democracy.

This red shirt protest rally comes at the end of a ten year struggle with a truly democratically elected government of the northern politician Thaksin Shinawatra. His understanding of democracy was shaped by his silk industry connections to government and his training as a police officer. His connections allowed him entry into government with information technology contracting and a profitable media empire he was building.

The Student Revolution of 37 years ago, launched a populist uprising that was repeatedly crushed, and yet survived to the real growth in 1992. The Democrat Party of central and southern Thailand assumed the mantel of leadership in the 1990s and were challenged by the north and northeast regions under Thaksin's astute leadership in 2001 until his personality revealed itself in the sale of the Shin Corporation (Broadcast media) and the **brutality** in the Muslim conflict of south Thailand.

---

260 *Bangkok Post*, Article by Wichit Chantanusornsiri, Business reporter, June 17, 2010.
261 *Bangkok Post*, Police reform panel chief appointed. June 30, 2010.

The Coup of 2006 and the Constitution of 2007[262] which was ratified by popular referendum, clearly showed Bangkok concurrence; the acts which transpired thereafter led first by the yellow shirted royalists with demonstrations and the airport take-overs, were followed by the Red shirts and their two-month rally in Bangkok, revealed an unwillingness to acknowledge the rights of rural Thais to participate in governance.

The failure of the police to participate in mob control until nearly the end of the Red-shirted rally reveal another dimension of Thai society: namely, the role of *classmate loyalty*, even stronger than national allegiance! Prime Minister Abhisit has created a Police Reform Panel and it will only succeed if he leads with total endorsement![263]

Amart and Prai: "The Prime Minister, the panelists and the organizers sat in the VIP reception room, chatting. The staff walked into the area, gave a bow and went to their knees. They crawled to the VIPs and served."[264] Here is a focus on inequality in society in India it is called *caste*, in Thailand it is simply accepted practice. A week later it is vibrating in the press as: **The Rich and the Poor.** "Thai elites have used this archaic form of ideology to keep a huge proportion of the population in virtual servitude." Aussie John

The problem is the lack of full participation. The cause of the problem is inequality and disparity. You see, when a man crawls to serve another man-what does that do to his spirit? But it is tradition, and society has been so conditioned to it for so long. We see nothing wrong with it. We don't even realize or recognize it. It's just the way things are.

"But what lies underneath is an amputated spirit, and unlike a lost arm or a lost leg, there is no prosthetic for it. Imagine a society, where

---

262 *Constitution of Thailand:* http://www.isaanlawyers.com/constitution%20thailand%20 2007%20-%202550.pdf (Courtesy: Prapan Disyatat, First Secretary, Royal Thai Embassy).
263 *Bangkok Post*, Police reform is a heavy task. July 22, 2010. Citing the statement of the Asian Human Rights Commission.
264 *Bangkok Post*, Commentary by Editor Voranai Vanijaka, July 18, 2010.

the majority has an amputated spirit."[265] Look around the room-the only ethnic Thais in here are me and the cameramen. The income gap that we are so focused on is merely a symptom. The cause of inequality and disparity is the state of mind, the condition of the spirit, the cultural psyche and attitude. The red shirts made a good point, even though they made it badlly. It's the amart (aristocrat) versus prai (ordianary people) dilemma.

"They know their place in society-and though they whine and cry about many things-they would never dream. They would never imagine that all of this can be changed. They are good Thais, they are good Buddhists-and this is Thailand, it's just the way it is."[266] **It's the cultural mentality, and that has to be changed-by bringing hope, inspiration and a sense of worthiness.**

Abhisit Vejjajiva insisted he was ready to be prime minister, and he has worked to understand the challenges into which he thrust himself. But, now he does see the demand for societal change to bring about a government **of the people, by the people and for the people** with an open and participatory election. This coming year will show how well Thailand is able to govern its society democratically.

Human Rights and Social Justice in Asia

The real struggle began in the Student-led Revolution in 1973, when the military dictators Field Marshals Prapat and Thanom were forced to leave the country after a Student-led Coup forced police and military into hiding as their university and technical training school students turned Bangkok into a War Zone and the traffic flows on the streets were managed by the Boy Scouts.

The students called upon the Monarch, King Bhumibol Adulyadej to establish a democratic government. The King appointed an academic

---

265 *Bangkok Post*, Commentary: Amart and Prai, July 18, 2010.
266 *Ibid*.

to head the government and then amazingly the King convened a unique assembly of citizens ranging across the entire society: farmers, taxi drivers, civil servants, military officers and police officials, businessmen and civic leaders to write a Constitution for this new government.[267] In essence, this monarch recognized all citizens as being part of the nation, and responsible for its governance.

Over the next twenty-five years several military coups occurred as had been a pattern since the first coup in December 1932. In 1992 the Monarch called the coup leaders to account on television and showed them they must not continue that coup pattern in the future.

In the election of 2001, a northern politician Thaksin Shinawatra, created a Party known as TRT, Thai Rak Thai, or Thais love Thais. This millionaire Police Colonel politician most effectively spoke to rural Thais of the North and Northeast and won easily over the Southern based Democratic Party that had held power. Thaksin proved to be an extremely effective populist politician while also inserting family and close associates into controlling positions throughout government.

Two principal issues seemingly caused intense dissatisfaction within the military and Bangkok society leading to the Coup of September 18, 2006 while Thaksin was out of the country in New York for the United nations General Assembly. Issue one: Thaksin had sold his Shin Corporation (broadcast media) to a Singapore-based Corporation and paid no taxes at all; Issue two: The Buddhist/Muslim conflict in South Thailand was being **brutally** suppressed by Thaksin and his Defense Ministry.

The Coup commander was a Thai/Muslim General Sonthi Boonyaratkalin, and the military held power while a Constitution was written and approved by referendum. Elections were held December 23, 2007 and the People's Power Party, successor to the banned TRT Party

---

[267] Along concepts from Fred Warren Riggs, Prismatic Theory of Society. *The Ecology of Public Administration*, New York: Asia Publishing House, 1961.

won a majority of the legislature and the struggle begins again between the Democratic Party and the Northern dominated PPP Successor to the TRT Party.[268]

Thailand's Human Rights & Social Justice Issues

The struggle between the People's Alliance for Democracy (PAD) also known as the "Yellow Shirts" and the United Front of Democracy against Dictatorship (UDD) also known as the "Red Shirts" was concluded in Bangkok in violent clashes from March 26 to May 19, 2010 by the Thai Army terminating the protests. Prime Minister Abhisit Vejjajiva has led the government toward a peaceful election wherein the Army would remain in the barracks and a reformed police force would carry on the control of the society as should be expected.

The Bangkok Post reported on October 29, 2010 the Udon Thani Provincial Court sentenced thirty-five red shirt defendants each to one year and eight months imprisonment for causing injury to supporters of the People's Alliance for Democracy at Nong Prachak public park on July 2008. And the red shirt defendants were applying for bail pending appeal.

As the cited case was being adjudicated the United Front of Democracy against Dictatorship (UDD) filed a petition with the National Anti-Corruption Commission (NACC) asking it to investigate and take legal action against four Constitution Court judges for nepotism. The petition named four judges: Boonsong Kulbuppha, Supoj Khaimuk, Chalempol Ek-uru, and Udomsk Nitimontree, who may have violated Articles 100(1), 152, and 157 of the Criminal Code regarding conflict of interests; and further contravening Article 279, paragraph 4 of the Constitution regarding judges' moral standards and thus could be removed from the Court according to Article 270.[269]

---

268 *Bangkok Post*, "The Race is On," August 28, 2007.
269 *Bangkok Post*, "UDD files suit against judges," October 29, 2010.

In the following week a YouTube video clip is shown by Puea Thai Party spokesman Prompong Noppart of Democrat Party MP Wirat Romyen discussing with Pasit Sakdanarong, a since-sacked secretary to Court president Chai Cholawrn, ways of helping the party out of trouble. In so doing Mr. Wirat had put the party under suspicion. Mr. Therdpong, Democrat Committee Chair, said Mr. Abhisit, Party Leader would decide how to handle the discipline of Mr. Wirat in this matter.[270]

Bangkok Metropolitan Administration is Building Flood Drainage Tunnels Under the City

A huge drainage tunnel system is being constructed to protect the city from annual threats of flooding in seasonal monsoons. Four tunnels are scheduled for completion in five years: the first tunnel, the Rama IX-Ramkhamhaeng, was begun ten years ago in eastern Bangkok to be completed in January 2011. The second tunnel, the Ratchada-phisek-Suthisarn, is expected to begin next year: with a diameter of 5 meters and a length of 6 kilometers. The third tunnel is the Don-Muang, with a diameter of 6 meters and a length of 13.5 kilometers. The last tunnel is the Rama IX Park Tunnel, with 6 meter diameter and length of 3 kilometers. MR Sukhumbhand said the system would increase the current drainage capacity from 95 cubic meters a second to 240 cubic meters a second. The tunnels will channel the floodwaters under Bangkok into the Chao Phraya River, which flows on into the Gulf of Thailand,[271] for 16 billion baht total cost.

Prime Minister Abhisit Vejjajiva responded to last week's tropical depression with assurances of aid that will be included in the government's flood relief scheme. The threat of flooding in the Chao Phraya River basin has eased significantly and the surrounding provinces must stay

---

270 *Bangkok Post*, "Democrat probe faults MP Wirat," November 2, 2010.
271 *Bangkok Post*, "BMA building flood drainage tunnel system," November 11, 2010.

alert, but conditions are improving. Heavy rains in the south caused parts of a mountain to collapse near Nakhon Si Thammarat. He promised aid to landslide victims, and would consider diverting funds for water retention areas and drainage canals.[272]

These comments of the Prime Minister Abhisit reveal how Thailand is responding to needs across the country in economic development terms. They will act to do work to protect the people, a sharp attitudinal change over fifty years! In 1975 Bangkok was flooded and people simply accepted that as fact! Now in 2010-11 they refuse to accept flooding and act to correct conditions to protect peoples' livelihoods.

Expanding Thai Industrial Development

The largest construction company in Thailand is Italian-Thai Development Plc (ITD) and they contract internationally. In April 2010 ITD announced it has signed a 10-year infrastructure development project with Burma for 240 billion baht on Burma's eastern coastline: covering a deep sea port, an industrial estate for heavy industries, and a connecting road and rail network.[273]

Thailand is finding itself limited by citizen actions to many industrial projects as in steel and petrochemicals, therefore, the Ministry of Industry announces a "roadshow" in Burma, to encourage investment between the two countries. Immediately Industry Minister Chaiwut Bannawat urges talks on food, processed rubber, and clothing. In the future investors should consider investing in iron smelting and petrochemical projects.[274]

---

272 *Bangkok Post*, "PM pledges aid to include storm victims," November 8, 2010.
273 *Bangkok Post*, "ITD signs Burma deal," April 11, 2010, and *Ibid*, "ITD says backlog value could swell to B300-400 billion," April 29, 2011.
274 *Bangkok Post*, "Industry roadshow to Burma this month," January 6, 2011; cf., *Ibid*, "Steel body proposes complex in Burma or Koh Kong," January 17, 2011.

Infrastructure Needs

The Burmese Earthquake of March 24, 2011 killed 74 Burmese and one Thai villager in Chiang Rai has stirred concerns about the safety of 2,700 city buildings in Bangkok. Many fault-lines exist in Thailand esp. along the border with Burma.[275] Both rail and highway infrastructure improvements were authorized by the Ministry of Transportation committee, with a budget total of 174 billion baht for upgrading existing rail and safety measures.[276]

Since the Yanhee Dam on the Ping River came on stream in November 1964, Thailand has developed a fast growing demand for electricity! Thailand has many hydropower projects, but the long discussed main steram Mekong Dam of the United Nations Committee failed to meet society demands at that time of the 1960-1970s. Since then China has built four dams on the upper Mekong in China and the flood control is now in full effect. Therefore it is not surprising to find that the Thai Government has contracted with the Laos Governement to buy electricity if a dam is built on the Mekong River. The Bangkok Post investigated and found much construction was underway, on a site at Xayaburi. The four member states of the Mekong River Commission (MRC): Cambodia, Laos, Thailand and Vietnam, are divided on whether the dam should be constructed.[277]

As all of this going on the Electricity Generating Authority of Thailand (Egat) has decided to build gas-fired power generators to replace thermal powered units scheduled to be replaced in Bangkok; and to delay any nuclear plants planned with a rethinking of nuclear development because of the events in Japan.[278] However, two months after this decision, a major gas line rupture undersea at the junction of

---

275 *Bangkok Post*, "2,700 city buildings at earthquake risk," March 26, 2011.
276 *Bangkok Post*, "Infrastructure development measures approved." April 11, 2011.
277 *Bangkok Post*, "Xayaburi dam work begins on sly," April 17, 2011 and May 8, 2011.
278 *Bangkok Post*, "Egat delays nuclear for gas," April 30, 2011.

a 34 inch and a 24 inch diameter pipe shuts down delivery for power plants and promises increased costs on billing.[279]

Just a Note on Thai Industrial Development

The Thailand Automotive Institute announced 2011 vehicle production is expected to total around 1.65 million units, a 10% drop due to the parts supply shortages caused by the Japanese earthquake and tsunami. Three major auto makers Toyota, Isuzu, and Honda Car, which between them have an 80 per cent of Thailand's domestic market, or about 800,000 units each year, will all be back in full production next month. It is expected that 2011 domestic car sales will be 850,000 units, with exports of between 750,000 and 800,000 units.[280]

Critical Thai Civil Rights Issues

At least 89 people died during the Bangkok Protest Violence April 10 to May 21, 2010 and each death is being investigated by the Department of Special Investigations (DSI). In a report on 18 of those deaths, DSI has concluded that UDD forces were responsible for 12 of those deaths. The other six deaths are not definitely determined, though the death of Japanese photo-journalist Hiyuki Muramoto would appear to have been caused by a shot from the military line.[281] The DSI is still investigating the deaths of the 71 others.

On Tuesday afternoon, March 15, 2011 the Truth and Reconciliation Commission (TRC) public forum on the death of Maj. Gen. Khattiya Sawasdpol "Seh Daeng" heard he was 58, a Potaram native and member of the 11th pre-cadet class, shot by a sniper on May 3, 2010 while being interviewed along Rama IV Road. The TRC forum was told that involved police officers had called to say they could not attend

---

279 *Bangkok Post*, "Pipeline leak will drive up power bills," says Egat," June 26, 2011.
280 *Bangkok Post*, "Auto output outlook 1.65m units in 2011," June 2, 2011.
281 *Bangkok Post*, "DSI 'botched probe into protest deaths," March 2, 2011.

without permission of their superiors. Mr. Somchai concluded that Seh Daeng was shot by a sniper, who must be either a decommissioned or a working officer, who must have been in one of the tall buildings nearby. (Bangkok Post, "TRC hears nothing new on Seh Daeng." 3/15/2011)

Urgent Need for Land Reforms

According to the Land Institute Foundation, about 6 million people or 10% of the population own 90% of the country's land. Yet 70% of these plots are speculative land left idle or under-used by absentee landlords. The economic damage from idle land is estimated at 127 billion baht a year. During 2007-08 alone, nearly 10,000 villagers were arrested and sent to jail. Many of them were forest dwellers arrested right on their ancestral lands. In the restive South, land rights conflicts with the Buddhist Thai state are among the chief resentments of the ethnic Malay Muslims there. Actually the fury of the masses has already been uleashed, resulting in the breakdown of consensus and endless political turmoil.[282]

On Tuesday February 1, 2011 the Cabinet approved the National Reform Committee's land reform proposals in principle. The proposals would set up a national land data base which would make people's land ownership public and further, it would restrict property ownership to 50 rai per family; establish a land bank to buy unused land and re-allocate it to landless farmers; imposing a progressive land tax to discourage large-scale landholding and zone land for agriculture.[283]

Farmers across Thailand are protesting: Ayutthaya, Chiang Mai, Ubon Ratchathani and in Bangkok that they are receiving no assistance from the government, and demand government action esp. to raise the guaranteed price of paddy to an acceptable level.[284]

---

282 *Bangkok Post, Asst. Editor Sanit* Ekachai, "Urgent need for land reform," February 10, 2011.
283 *Bangkok Post*, "Cabinet approves land reform proposals," February 15, 2011.
284 *Bangkok Post*, "Ayutthaya farmers block Asian highway," March 17, 2011, and *Ibid.*, "Farmers demand urgent govt action," April 26, 2011.

Thailand's southern Malay Muslims are not ignorant, rather highly educated in Muslim traditions and values. That is a direct conflict with Thai education offered in southern Thailand. They learn three languages, Malay, Thai and Arabic and are strictly trained in their faith traditions. Therefore the problem will not be solved by education, nor by job offers necessarily; rather, thorough political decentralization would appear to be the only possible solution to the southern conflicts.[285]

As the House has passed the first public assembly law, both groups, PAD and UDD are planning rallies in Bangkok on the anniversary of last years March-May protest.

> **Jatuporn Prompan, a Puea Thai list MP and very vocal co-leader of the United Front for Democracy against Dictatorship (UDD), pointed the finger at the army. He claimed some 'hooded men who are more powerful than the police and the military' had thrown bombs into CentralWorld shopping mall and set fire to the building.**
>
> **The accusation drew a sharp rebuke from Army Commander-in-Chief General Prayuth Chan-cha.**

Air Force Commander-in-Chief ACM Ithiporn Supawong joined in "Think about it, about the men in black who had guns. Who actually burned it down.[286]

Need for Truth and Reconciliation

The Chulalongkorn University Seminar on "Organizations and Process on Reconciliation After the election," agreed that any post election government **must** allow the continuation of the Truth and Reconciliation Commission for Thailand (TRCT) to continue its vital

---

285 *Bangkok Post*, Asst. Editor Sanitsuda Ekachai, "South needs the power to fix woes," March 10, 2011.
286 *Bangkok Post*, Verra Prateepchaikul, Former Editor, "Weekly Highlights" March 11, 2011.

work in resolving conflicts within the Thailand Society. "We need a social contract from all political groups that the TRCT will be given the necessary independence, resources, and cooperation."[287]

Samut Sakhon Province Coal-Mining Conflicts

The Central Administrative Court ordered a temporary halt to transportation and storage of coal in depots and processing facilities within local communities. The order was issued four days after the murder of environmental activist Thongnak Sawekchinda. The owner of a coal-trucking company and four suspects have been arrested and a petition has been filed by citizens of the province to have the governor removed for dereliction of duty by allowing the transport of coal which has caused the pollution of the Tha Chin river and destroyed the environment, and of failing to take action against coal barges and shipping ports.[288]

His Majesty the King Urges Compassion

In His New Year's Message the King said in a televised speech that everyone shared the same Wish – to be happy and to progress in life. We also wish the country to be peaceful and the people should offer love, compassion, and kindness to each other. They also should forgive and come to the aid of each other in their hour of need. His Majesty emphasized that people should treat each other with good faith and sincere and honest intentions. This is so that everyone can come together and as a collective force, figure out how to create happiness, prosperity, and security for themselves and the nation.[289]

---

287 *Bangkok Post*, "Truth commission" 'still needed,' June 21, 2011.
288 *Bangkok Post*, "Thongnak did not die in vain, August 2, 2011, and *Ibid*. "Coal protestors want Samut Sakhon governor out," August 4, 2011.
289 *Bangkok Post*, "HM urges compassion," December 31, 2010.

Tormenting Issues Afflicting Thai Society

Bare-breasted culture of hypocrisy: Three teen aged girls 14 to 16 years of age responded to urging of on-lookers on Silom Road during Songkram celebrations danced topless on a pickup truck to the cheers of spectators. And then the Culture Minister Niphit Intharasombat lambasted the teenagers for offending the country's culture. While his Culture Ministry website had displayed three bare-breasted women for many years.

The Bang Rak district chief had the nerve to press for the girls' arrest for "destroying the country's reputation." While it is his district that embraces the notorious *Patpong!* The police fined the girls each 500 baht for their offense.[1]

The Bang Rak district chief had the nerve to press for the girls' arrest for "destroying the country's reputation." While it is his district that embraces the notorious *Patpong!* The police fined the girls each 500 baht for their offense.[290]

---

290 *Bangkok Post*, "Analysing the bare facts," April 19, 2011, and *Ibid*, "Bare-breasted culture of hypocrisy," April 20, 2011.

Cambodia's Khao Preah Vihear Temple

The International Court of Justice rendered a judgement June 15, 1962, awarding Cambodia the Temple of Preah Vihear based upon a map published by Thailand showing boundary lines for Cambodia including the Temple grounds. Conservative forces in Thailand have never accepted that decision. Ultra-activist PAD yellow-shirted Thai Patriot Network (TPN) members entered Cambodian territory near a military area and were arrested. Seven were detained in Prey Sar Prison under Phnom Penh Municipal Court control. In Bangkok their supporters launched a petition effort to win the endorsement of His Majesty the King for the release of those TPN members held in Cambodia.[291] And bail was granted to all but Verra Somkhwamkid a coordinator for the TPN, who had had previous incidents of illegal entry.[292]

The rally in Bangkok is coordinated by the People's Alliance for Democracy (PAD) and they reject the government's proposal for negotiations to end the road-blocking rally. "It is not time for talks. The government should comply with our demands," Maj. Gen. Chamlong Srimuang. The PAD position demands Thailand's withdrawal from the Unesco World Heritage Committee, the revocation of the 2000 MoU signed with Cambodia and ejecting Cambodians in border areas the group claims belong to Thailand back to their homeland.[293] Inflaming all of these demonstrations is the fact that flags of Cambodia and Thailand are flying in disputed areas of the Temple, and soldiers of both sides have been killed in exchanges between armed forces.

Cambodia filed a request to the International Court of Justice for legal clarification to settle the border dispute around the Preah Vihear

---

[291] *Bangkok Post*, "Court slaps 2 Thais with spying charges," January 10, 2011, and *Ibid.*, 'TPN's Chaiwat files petition, then arrested, "January 18, 2011.
[292] *Bangkok Post*, "Verra denied bail in Cambodia, others released," January 18, 2011.
[293] *Bangkok Post*, "Just do as we demand, PAD tells govt." January 28, 2011.

temple and the ICJ has accepted that request, so that both sides are now preparing their legal positions.[294]

Thai Defense Minister Prawit Wongsuwon said the ICJ had "no authority" to issue an order to withdraw troops from the border area disputed with Cambodia. That view was contradicted by Foreign Minister Kasit Piromya upon returning from a two-day ICJ oral hearing in the Hague that the Court has enforcement power, but as a good UN member country, Thailand would comply with its decision.[295]

Thailand debates withdrawing from the Unesco World Heritage Committee (WHC), but PM Abhisit delays action until a new government is formed.[296] However, Foreign Ministry officials led a survey team of Indonesian officials to the Temple site in preparation for an Indonesian Observer Team (IOT) expected soon according to an army source." The IOT will have 15 members. Most of them Indonesian soldiers, but they will be wearing civilian clothes."[297]

"The International Court of Justice on Monday voted 11 to 5 to order both Thailand and Cambodia to withdraw their troops from the 4.6 square kilometer disputed area around the Preah Vihear temple to reduce military confrontation along their border."[298]

In its order, the Court first unanimously rejected Thailand's request for the case introduced by Cambodia to be removed from the General List, meaning that the Court retains the authority to consider the Cambodian request. The Court also stated with 15 votes to 1 that Thailand should not obstruct Cambodia's free access to Preah Vihear Temple, or prevent it from providing fresh supplies to its nonmilitary personnel. The Court said that Cambodia and Thailand should continue their cooperation within the Association of Southeast Asian Nations and, in particular, allow

---

294 *Bangkok Post*, "Abhisit says govt ready for ICJ petition defense," April 4, 2011, and *Ibid*, Head of legal team to ICJ named," May 4, 2011.
295 *Bangkok Post*, "Thailand set to defy any border order," Jun 5, 2011.
296 *Bangkok Post*, "PM backs withdrawal from WHC," June 26, 2011.
297 *Bangkok Post*, "Indonesian survey team taken to border," July 6, 2011.
298 *Bangkok Post*, "ICJ orders troops withdrawn, "July 18, 2011.

the observers appointed by that organization to have access to the provisional demilitarized zone, and that both parties should refrain from any action which might aggravate or extend the dispute before the Court or make it more difficult to resolve. Lastly, the Court decided, with 15 votes to 1, that each of the parties should inform the Court as to its compliance to the above provisional measures and that, until the Court has rendered its judgement on the request for interpretation, it would remain seised of the matters which form the subject of the order.[299]

---

299 *Bangkok Post*, "Remove military from temple area – ICJ," July 19, 2011, and *Ibid.*, "Asean welcomes ICJ move," July 19, 2011.

Chapter XIII

Moving Toward a Democratic Election

From The Democratic Party's Perspective

Ms. Suu Kyi Aung San and Thaksin Shinawatra are like *heaven and hell.* After the Burmese government released Ms. Suu Kyi from detention, Thaksin launched a press statement that Thai reconciliation would begin after political detainees are release. Democrat MP Attaporn Poniaboot said if Thaksin were sincere, while he was in office he would have urged the Burmese release of Ms. Suu Kyi rather than negotiate benefits for his son and network.[300]

At the end of November 2010 the Constitution Court returned a verdict that dismissed charges of electoral fraud against the Democrat Party. PM Abhisit moved quickly to urge a meeting with the PAD leadership to resolve issues like the Preah Vihear temple and planned rallies in January 2011. He assigned the Center for Resolution of the Emergency Situation to coordinate with the UDD on their planned rally December 10th.[301] The Emergency Decree was initially imposed in 24 provinces in the wake of the protests by the red-shirts of the

---

300 *Bangkok Post*, "Dems: Thaksin's comment misleading," November 14, 2010.
301 *Bangkok Post*, "PM: Time to get back to work," November 29, 2010, and *Ibid.*, PM still wants to meet PAD leaders," December 3, 2010.

United Front for Democracy against Dictatorship. It is still in place in Bangkok, Pathum Thani, Nonthaburi and Samut Prakan. Politics remains dangerously polarized at the start of an election year.[302]

The government promised a process of 'reconciliation' after the killings in May, but there is little sign of one. Even the best-mannered of the Thai government's critics, let alone the radicals on the northeast, survive in an atmosphere of fear and intimidation. The government is required to hold general elections before the end of 2011. The conservative coalition government of Abhisit Vejjajiva of the Democrat Party is far from secure as it begins its third year in office. Openly red policemen are called tomatoes; only a slightly smaller proportion of soldiers are of the same viewpoint and though dressed in green on the outside but red at the core, these troops are called watermelons.[303]

Democrat Party launches Thailand Reform Plan

PM aims to improve the quality of life for Thais, riddling the country of corruption and creating good governance nationwide. Encourage breastfeeding, open pre-school facilities, promotion of land-ownership, low-interest loans and cheap health insurance for motorcycle taxi and taxi drivers.[304] Implementation of these programs for Thais will be beneficial for the Democrat Party in the next election, and they should win the largest number of seats in its history.[305]

The Democrat Party is essentially a central and southern Thai party and not one fully aware of the problems of the northeast. The Pak Moon dam built at the confluence of the Moon river and the Mekong river in Ubon Ratchathani in 1994 has been a total failure, simply because the

---

302 *Bangkok Post*, "PM: Emergency rule could be lifted before New Year," December 8, 2010.
303 *The Economist*, "Beware the watermelons: Thailand's red-shirt opposition," January 1, 2011, p. 33.
304 *Bangkok Post*, "Scheme will boost education, stem graft," January 2, 2011.
305 *Bangkok Post*, "Abhisit prefers early dissolution of House," January 3, 2011.

fishing communities have fought it and have delayed its operations year after year. The Abhisit administration dropped the proposal to leave the sluice gates open for five years and then possibly decommission the dam. With that refusal to support the people of the Pak Moon community all votes are lost.[306]

The confident PM Abhisit announces to the Election Commission members that he will dissolve the House in early May 2011, for an election in late June or early July. PM Abhisit said he will propose during the House meeting tomorrow that the three bills drawn up by the Election Commission be made a top priority and moved up the House agendas for urgent deliberation. If the bills pass the first reading tomorrow, a joint Senate-MP committee will be set up to scrutinize the bills. This will take about two weeks. They will then go through the second and third readings before being passed in preparation for an early general election. The three bills govern elections of MPs and senators, political parties, and the operation of the Election Commission.[307]

Government Enters Its Final Week

Prime Minister Abhisit Vejjajiva confirmed he has submitted a royal decree seeking a House dissolution to His Majesty the King for royal endorsement.[308] Caretaker prime minister and Democrat Party leader Abhisit hit the campaign trail in the North, focusing on key policy issues affecting communities in protected forest areas and occupying public lands, assuring that land title deeds will be allowed for agricultural land use. In Chiang Mai he spoke to those who were benefiting from Democrat Party land policies. In Phayao province he drew a crowd of 4,000 in a stronghold of the Pheu Thai Party.[309]

PM Abhisit has stated his opposition to the Pheu Thai proposal for

---

306 *Bangkok Post*, "Democrats lose Pak Moon vote," February 25, 2011.
307 *Bangkok Post*, "Suthep: House dissolution by May 10," March 22, 2011.
308 *Bangkok Post*, "PM: I've kept my promise," May 6, 2011.
309 *Bangkok Post*, "Abhisit hits campaign trail in North today," June 1, 2011.

an Amnesty referendum for all offenses committed after the 2006 coup, saying it was probably not constitutional.[310]

The **Abac** poll of May 2, 2011, conducted by Assumption University, showed Abhisit well in the lead, however a month later, the poll by the Special branch police conducted in 331 of the 375 constituencies nation-wide, not including Bangkok and the three southernmost of Yala, Pattani, and Narathiwat showed the Democrats had fallen behind their rival the Pheu Thai. Abhisit has admitted they are behind but not far back and challenging. He said that the Pheu Thai will not gain a landslide victory at the July 3 election.[311]

The Democrats will proceed with a Thursday, June 23 rally at the Ratchaprasong intersection even though business interests wished to be spared the attention. And the red-shirts had decided they would not do anything to counter the rally. Abhisit will point out what problems are lying ahead for us, and some of the things that must be done to lead the nation forward. Tomorrow's rally is being seen as the final big gamble by the Democrats to sway the minds of Bangkok's undecided voters to cast their ballots in favor of their party, which has fallen far behind the Pheu Thai Party in almost all the opinion polls conducted in the past few weeks. These voters will be reminded of the chain of events last year, particularly the looting and burning spree on the last day of the riot, and who were actually responsible for these criminal acts[312].

Peoples Alliance for Democracy Asks EC to Dissolve Pheu Thai Party

The PAD said in the petition that since ousted premier Thaksin is under a five year political ban and also a fugitive after being sentenced to imprisonment, The Pheu Thai Party, by implementing his orders, had violated Sections 68 and 237 of the constitution, Articles 53, 137

---

310 *Bangkok Post*, "Abhisit opposes referendum plan," June 10, 2011.
311 *Bangkok Post*, "PM insists election race is still close," June 12, 2011.
312 *Bangkok Post*, "PM insists election race is still close," June 12, 2011.

and 159 of the Election of MPs and Senators Act, and Articles 4, 66, and 94 of the Political Party Act. And therefore, the Pheu Thai Party should be dissolved.[313]

At the same time, Abhisit has called upon the leading opponent of the Pheu Thai Party, Yingluck Shinawatra, Thaksin's youngest sister to clarify her relationship with the red-shirted UDD members who are heckling him at his rallies. She has tended to brush aside his concerns and on this occasion of her 44th birthday she was up early to offer food to monks in their morning rounds.[314]

Democrat Party Offers Banned Politicians Amnesty

Jumping on the amnesty bandwagon, the Democrats offer banned politicians' amnesty for violating the Election Law. More than 200 people are currently banned from politics. Some of those under the ban have been key supporters of new parties, including Newin Chidchob of Bhumjaithai, Banharn Silpa-archa of Charthaipattana and Suwat Liptapanlop of Chart Pattana Pusa Pandin.[315] And of course, though not cited because of his other convictions for illegal activities, Thaksin Shinawatra of the Puea Thai Party.

From the Puea Thai Party Perspective

The Puea Thai Party image might gain from the proposed membership of a royal family member, namely, Maj. Gen. Mom Chao Chulcherm Yugala, as suggested by Gen. Chavalit Yongchaiyudh, the party's advisory chairman and former prime minister. Honestly, even if MC Chulcherm or any other members of the royalty were to join Puea

---

313 *Bangkok Post*, "PAD asks EC to dissolve P. Thai," June 21, 2011.
314 *Bangkok Post*, "Abhisit: Yingluck should clarify support for UDD," June 21, 2011.
315 *Bangkok Post*, "Democrats offer amnesty plan: would repeal political bans for more than 200," June 25, 2011.

Thai, it would not help much in dispelling the widespread belief that the party is not loyal to the monarchy.[316]

The December 11th Bangkok Puea Thai rally went well and the voting surprised everyone when the weekend poll defeats in Surin, Nakhon Ratchasima, and Ayutthaya are clearly a cause of concern for the Puea Thai Party. Hence, an urgent meeting was called by the party leadership to find out what went wrong with its campaign, to assess the damage and to work out measures to right the wrongs. However, the poll outcome does speak volumes of one thing; that a medium size political party like Bhumjaithai and Chart Thai Pattana have a better chance of competing with the big parties such as the Puea Thai in a smaller constituency; which explains why the Constitution had to be amended to change the electoral system from multi-MP constituencies to single-MP constituencies.[317]

No matter where he is, Thaksin obviously has to carefully and thoroughly think over who will be the new leader of the party he backs. Youngyuth Wichaidit is in the driver's seat, but the former career bureaucrat is obviously under-qualified to drive the opposition party when a new general election comes. A more serious problem for Thaksin is nobody having been in the news is good enough to sell to voters. They want to see a candidate from Puea Thai who is good enough to be prime minister in case the party is lucky to win the election.[318]

The red-shirt rally for March 12th was promised to be peaceful! The course was to begin at the Democracy Monument on Ratchadamnoen Avenue, then head to the Phan Fa Bradge, Nakhon Sawan Road,

---

316 *Bangkok Post*, "Recruiting royalty wouldn't improve Puea Thai's image," November 16, 2010.
317 *Bangkok Post*, "Has Thaksin really lost his magic touch in the Nartheast?" December 14, 2010, and *Ibid*. "Charter changes to King tomorrow," February 23, 2011.
318 *Bangkok Post*, "Thaksin is paying for his arrogance," January 3, 2011.

Pitsanulok Road, Phetchaburi Road, Phratunam intersection, and then to Ratchaprasong intersection.[319]

Economist Mingkwan Sangsuwan, Puea Thai MP, said the party would attack PM Abhisit for hislack of ideas to get the nation moving economically, to boost economic growth. When asked about the proposal that Yingluck Shinawara, younger sister of Thaksin, would be supported for the role of Puea Thai leader and possibly become the country's first female prime minister, the MP said he had no idea who floated that story.[320] The Criminal Court approved the release of eight men who had been held for a year on terrorism-related charges stemming from the political violence in April and May of 2010. They included: Weng Tojirakam, Natthawut Saikua, Korkaew Pikulthong, Wiphuthalaeng Pattanaphumthai, Yossawaris Chuklom or Jeng Dokchik, Nisit Srithuprai and Kwanchai Sarakham, who will be on stage at the red-shirt rally. House Speaker Chai Chidchob said that the release of UDD leaders was good for all parties involved.[321]

Continuing his attacks on the Democrat Party, MP Mingkwan Saengsuwan, Puea Thai leader focused on the government's mismanagement of the economy. This led into a censure debate, with the onslaught carried by Puea Thai MP Jatuporn Prompan accusing Mr. Abhisit and Deputy Prime Minister in charge of security affairs Suthep Thaugsuban of being murderers for ordering the crackdown on the protestors. Jatuporn spent about three hours Thursday night painting Mr. Abhisit, Mr. Suthep and the military as the sole villains and red-shirt protestors as innocent people struggling for democracy.[322]

At this same time, the Commerce Minister reported exports rose to US$18.86 billion in February on a year-on-year basis, with imports

---

319 *Bangkok Post*, "Red-shirts promise to rally in peace," January 8, 2011.
320 *Bangkok Post*, "Mingkwan: Abhisit prime target," February 2, 2011.
321 *Bangkok Post*, "Freed red leaders to return on stage," February 23, 2011.
322 *Bangkok Post*, Verra Prateepchaikul, Former Editor, "Weekly highlights," March 18, 2011.

at US$17.1 billion, thus a February trade surplus of US$1.768 billion. The Finance Ministry projected a fiscal year tax collection to exceed the targeted 1.2 trillion baht.[323]

Criteria for Leadership

The deposed former premier lays down criteria!

1) The candidate must be courteous, modest and able to work with all sides without constantly making enemies.
2) The candidate must have compassion.
3) The candidate must abide by justice.
4) The candidate must have courage to correct mistakes.
5) The candidate must understand the people's economy and the business sector.
6) The candidate must have experience managing major organizations, as knowledge alone is not enough.
7) The candidate must love the people.
8) The candidate must love democracy and respect people's capabilities and intelligence.
9) The candidate must adhere to the country's constitutional monarchy.

This set of criteria is a credit to Mr. Thaksin Shiawatra, for these are the qualities needed as Mr. Suthep Thaugsuban, Deputy Prime Minister says, only his Democrat and the Puea Thai Party candidates meet these criteria.[324]

These comments by former Prime Minister Thaksin Shinawatra clearly reveal his reflections on his mistakes in governing prior to being couped by the Thai military in 2006. It gives credit to the academic work

---

323 *Bangkok Post*, "February exports up 31%," March 18, 2011.
324 *Bangkok Post*, "Thaksin sets criteria for P. Thai leaader," March 21, 2011.

he did in earning his M.A. in criminal justice at Eastern Kentucky University and Ph.D. at San Houston State University in 1979.

In an interview with the Wall Street Journal, from his residence in Dubai, Thaksin says he plans to influence Thai Government if the Puea Thai Party wins the election and he is focused on issues like: cutting corporate tax rates and granting amnesty to all people charged with politically related offences since the military coup that ousted his government in September 2006. Meanwhile, the pro-Thaksin UDD plans to file a civil law suit demanding 39.8 million baht compensation for damages on behalf of 16 red-shirts who were killed or wounded in the clash between soldiers and the UDD protestors at the Khok Wua intersection on April 10, last year. The suit would be against three agencies as defendants: the Finance Ministry, the Defense Ministry and the army, under the law concerning offenses committed by state officials.[325]

Thai authorities forced the closure of 13 antigovernment radio stations yesterday in the biggest crackdown on dissident media since a state of emergency during street protests last year. The anti-government red-shirt movement said stations based in Bangkok and its suburbs were raided by law enforcement. When last year's demonstrations aimed at toppling Abhisit's the government was to try to shut down their media network, including community radio stations. The military is said to fear the return to power of allies of former prime minister Thaksin Shinawatra, whom it deposed in a 2006 coup amid accusations that he was corrupt and had showed disrespect to constitutional monarch King Bhumibol Adulyadej.[326]

Constitution Court Approves Election-Related Bills

The Court unanimously approved the three election bill clearing the way for the general election. The three bills govern election of

---

325 *Bangkok Post*, "Thaksin confirms his role in Puea Thai," April 8, 2011.
326 *The Boston Globe*, "Thailand shuts dissident radio stations," April 27, 2011.

MPs and senators, political parties, and the operation of the Election Commission. His Majesty the King has issued a royal command to dissolve the House of Representatives tomorrow, May 10.[327]

In one form or another, Thaksin Shinawatra has been in the thick of Thai politics for a decade. Since September 2006, when the two-term prime minister was ousted in a coup, he has had to rely on proxies to fight his corner. And so, on July 3rd, Mr. Thaksin's youngest sister, Yingluck Shinawatra, will be his stand-in when Thais vote in the first national election since December 2007.

The red-shirts' battle cry was for new elections. Now that the prime minister, Abhisit Vejjajiva, has dissolved parliament, some wonder if the process might somehow be derailed. The ultranationalist, and anti-Thaksin, yellow-shirts have called for an appointed royalist government to clean up politics. Asked about coup plots, military chiefs serve up boilerplate denials, just as they did in 2006.[328]

The Puea Thai Party has lodged a complaint with the Election Commission accusing Kaewsun Atibhodhi and Tul Sithisomwong of breaching the election law. The Party contends the accused are attempting to smear Ms. Yingluck Shinawatra linking her to the case against her brother Thaksin Shinawatra. The EC secretary-general Suthiphon Thaveechaiyagarn said the agency would treat the Puea Thai Party petition like any other complaint. He said the agency has to be very discreet when dealing with complaints because the election campaign is intensifying.[329]

Mr. Noppadon Pattana a close aide to Thaksin said the party would not pursue amnesty but was interested in 'reconciliation' for victims of injustice. The bottom line is who these victims of injustice

---

327 *Bangkok Post*, "Court Clears election bills," May 9, 2011.
328 *The Economist*, "Thailand's Politics: Thaksin's last stand," June 4, 2011, p. 47.
329 *Bangkok Post*, "Puea Thai claims smear plot: EC urged to investigate those targeting Yingluck," June 8, 2011.

are. Who are the ones affected by the wrongful orders of those who seized power?³³⁰

On the Campaign Trail

Just before leaving for Phitsanulok. Ms. Yingluck commented on the Democrats changed rally location,"…hoped the Democrat Party's major rally at the Ratchaprasong intersection on June 23 would be constructive." The Democrats, led by party leader Abhisit Vejjajiva, went on a campaign trail in Samut Prakan on Sunday morning.³³¹

The Bangkok Post, feels that when you want to know how the people feel talk to the 'brother' taxi driver or the 'auntie' merchant in the market. The cab driver continues, "For party list, I will vote Chuwit. But for individual constituency, I will vote Puea Thai. 80 to 90 percent of people like me will always support Puea Thai." "Why is that 'brother'?" He paused for a moment, looked in the rear view mirror and said, "There's no reason. It's in here. He tapped the left side of his chest, "It's in the heart." Please explain 'brother' what do you mean? The cab driver told of how life is just easier with Puea Thai in control. Making a living is easier. Everything just seems easier. There's a trust. There's a relationship. When a Puea Thai MP talks to you, you understand what he or she is saying. He or she is speaking the language of the people.

"Yingluck hasn't done anything and she won't have to do anything. She only has to look pretty, smile, gives hugs and handshakes and photos. She doesn't have to speak with substance, only as a daughter or a sister, friendly and personable, and the Yingluck fever rages on. She already has the human touch. Just take a look at her on the campaign trail. She's comfortable. She's confident. She's in tune." The **human**

---

330 *Bangkok Post*, "Puea thai unveals 'justice panel,'" June 18, 2011.
331 *Bangkok Post*, "Yingluck hopes Dems constructive," June 19, 2011.

touch, perhaps they don't teach it at Oxford, perhaps they do at Sam Houston State or Kentucky State.³³²

International Media Takes Notice of the Thai Election

In a recent televised debate hosted by the BBC, Mr Abhisit accused Thaksin and his candidates of wanting to "subvert the rule of law" by granting himself amnesty. "If you love my brother, will you give his youngest sister a chance?" She routinely asks the crowds at her campaigning events across the country, according to the Associated Press. The answer is always a resounding "Yes."³³³

The leading parties use wildly generous campaigns to win voters in a campaign with more than 40 parties contending. None of the lead parties are campaigning for integrity or fiscal responsibility. On the other hand the newcomers, such as Rak Santi (Love Peace) and Rak Prathetthai (Love Thailand) parties are banking on integrity and do not emphasize populism. The contrast suggests both change and continuity in Thai electoral politics. For the protagonists, such as the Democrats, Puea Thai, Bhumjathai, Chart Pattana Puea Pandin and Chart Thai Pattana parties, their brands of populism run the gamut. Puea Thai pledges 10 mass transit rail lines for a flat commuter price of 20 baht, computers for children, minimum wage hikes, tax rebates on first homes and first cars, free internet in public areas, one scholarship for foreign study per district, credit cards for farmers, among other. This is another contrast that may be pointing to a newly emerging, but still inchoate political landscape, where parties are forced to cater to voters' demands and expectations in ways not seen in decades past.³³⁴

---

332 *Bangkok Post*, Commentary by Voranai Vanijaka, "Building by Persuasion," June 19, 2011.
333 *The Washington Times*, "Exiled leader's sister runs for Thailand prime minister," June 24, 2011.
334 *Bangkok Post*, Opinion of thitinan Pongsudhirak, Director, ISIS, Chulalongkorn Univ., June 18, 2011.

Southern Thailand Arena of Conflict

Regardless of which party wins the election, they must deal with the Muslim conflict in the four southern provinces. The Southern Border Provinces Administration Center (SBPAC) re-established by the Abhisit government must be utilized to help ease conflict in the four provinces. Thaksin Shinawatra while prime minister sidelined the body, because he wanted to give his cousin and army commander, Gen Chaisit Shinawatra control of the forces in the south. *Under Thaksin this was a disaster.* The army mishandled events badly, including the killing of more than 125 men in the infamous Krue Sa mosque and Tak Bai incidents. The violent insurgency in the south is not simple to solve. Southerners have spoken with their voices and their actions; they do not like dealing with the security forces. The Center can deal with complaints, and it is empowered to dismiss even high-ranking officials who abuse their power, the people or both.[335]

Thailand's General Election

The surge of enthusiasm for PT owes a lot not only to Mr. Thaksin's enduring popularity among Thailand's rural poor, but also to the dizzying rise of the official party leader, his younger sister Yingluck, who was unknown only a month or so ago. A fresher face even than the relatively youthful 47-year old Mr. Abhisit, and a woman campaigning in the very male world of Thai politics, she has injected a buzz and excitement into the election. Her seasoned, pragmatic campaign managers have exploited her looks and easy-going nature to the fullest. She, for her part, has played the perfect candidate by sticking closely to her sound bites and smiling ceaselessly at the camera.[336]

The Electral Commission has invited 10 countries to send

---

335 *Bangkok Post*, Editorial, "The power of the rule of law," April 6, 2011.
336 *The Economist*, "Lucky Yingluck," June 25th, 2011, p. 51.

representative to observe the election: Australia, Bangladesh, Bhutan, India, South Korea, Malaysia, Maldives, Nepal, Switzerland, and Japan. And the United Nations Secretary General Ban Ki-Moon has called for a crucial general election in Thailand to be conducted peacefully and in a "fair, credible and transparent" way.[337]

Rival parties achieve different feel for rain-soaked closings, with Democrats struggling to emote, and Pheu Thai's concert-like meet failing to sizzle. The evening downpour may have spoiled the party mood at the final rallies of the two major parties, but the show did go on.[338]

As the Bangkok Post, said on the morning of July 4th, "It is a landslide". Thai Prime Minster Abhisit Vejjajiva conceded on Sunday evening that his party had lost the national elections to the opposition led by Yingluck Shinawatra. The election paves the way for Ms. Yingluck to become Thailand's first female prime minister. With 80 percent of the vote counted, official results indicated Ms. Yingluck's Phue Thai party would win 251 seats, just over the majority needed to form a government.[339]

Within a week Yingluck is able to announce a further strengthening of her position with a coalition of other parties to total MP numbers to 300, with Chartthaipattana, Chart Pattana Puea Pandin, Palang Chon, and Mahachon parties. And she further announces that knowledge and competence are the criterion for selection to serve in the cabinet and that qualified red-shirts would be eligible.[340]

---

337 *Bangkok Post*, "UN chief wants credible election," June 30, 2011.
338 *Bangkok Post*, "Final rallies fail to hit high note," July 2, 2011.
339 *The Washington Times*, "Thai prime minister concedes election to ousted leader's sister," July 3, 2011, and *The Washington Post*, "5 years after Thailand coup, ousted PM Thaksin's sister wins elections with proxy party," July 3, 2011.
340 *Bangkok Post*, "Yingluck: Reds can serve in cabinet," July 7, 2011.

Democrats Seek P.T. Dissolution

Democrat Party's legal team member Wirat Kallayasiri initiated legal action to seek the dissolution of the Puea Thai Party, filing a complaint with the Election commission about the involvement of banned politicians. The outgoing ruling party asked the Election Commission to recommend that the Puea Thai Party, which won the July 3 general election, be disbanded on the grounds that banned politicians were involved in the election campaign. Mr. Wirat said, some of the 111 executive members of the dissolved Thai Rak Thai Party who were banned from politics for five years in 2008, including ousted premier Thaksin Shinawatra and TRT deputy leader Chaturon Chaisang, have been more involved in P.T. activities than the actual P.T. executive members. Article 97 of the constitution clearly states that executives from any disbanded party are prohibited from being involved with any other party during the suspension period.[341]

Prime minister in-waiting Yingluck Shinawatra denied the charge, saying Puea Thai have working teams to map out policies to settle pressing problems of the country.[342]

These conflicting challenges are legal and healthy! As Jean-Jacques Rousseau put it, "A little bit of agitation gives motivation to the soul, and what really makes the species prosper is not peace so much as freedom. With freedom comes some unpredictable fluctuation. This is one of life's packages: there is no freedom without noise – and no stability without volatility."

Thailand's prime minister-to-be said yesterday that she would try to benefit from her exiled brother's ideas to help the country but insisted she will make her own decisions as leader and not be his puppet. Yingluck said she would make decisions for the country independently. She parried many questions about her planned policies, preferring to

---

341 *Bangkok Post*, "Democrats seek Puea Thai's dissolution," July 8, 2011.
342 *Bangkok Post*, "Yingluck denies Thaksin's involvement," July 9, 2011.

wait until she takes office. She said her 20 years of business experience have shown she can make her own decisions, but she will consult with the Puea Thai Party leaders who helped her to victory and with the Cabinet she appoints. Yingluck is set to become prime minister after she is elected by the members of the Parliament when they convene later this month, though some last-ditch legal efforts are challenging her election victory.[343]

Election Commission Acts

On Tuesday, July 12th the EC endorsed only 358 of the 500 MP-elect, in both the constituency and party-list systems. They said more would be endorsed on July 19th and at least 475 MPs would be endorsed by August 3rd so that the new House of Representatives can convene within the 30 days of election day as required by the law.[344]

Yingluck insisted that she is the sole Puea Thai candidate for prime minister and that party leader Yongyuth Wichaidit is not in-waiting for the post if she is not endorsed by the EC. The first hurdle for the youngest sister of ousted prime minister Thaksin Shinawatra is proving she is playing a part in assigning cabinet posts instead of letting her brother control the arrangements. She also has to contend with interference from close associates, including Thaksin's former wife Khunying Potjaman na Pombeya, and her elder sister Yaowapa Wongsawat and her husband Somchai, who are trying to usher members of their own factions into the cabinet. In addition to that, red-shirt members of her party are demanding at least two cabinet posts from her as a reward for their success in bringing in 22-party list members and another 10 constituency representative to parliament.[345]

---

[343] *The Boston Globe*, "New Thai leader says she won't be puppet," July 9, 2011.
[344] *Bangkok Post*, "EC to endorse more MPs on July 19," July 13, 2011.
[345] *Bangkok Post*, "Yingluck's uphill battle: Political newcomer has to rise above meddling brother, demanding red-shirts," July 16, 2011.

Both Yingluck and Abhisit are cleared of poll complaints and unanimously endorsed by the commissioners of the EC. The EC also certified 10 other elected candidates, including Suthep Thaugsuban, Chinnicha Wongsuwat and Thanin Jaisamut. Other MP-elects including leaders of the UDD had not yet been endorsed.[346]

Yingluck Shinawatra: Sister Act

For her part she acknowledges that she learned her 'thinking and management style' from him but insists nonetheless, 'I will lead." Indeed, after her spectacular victory, Ms. Yingluck has amassed her own political capital, regardless of big brother. Just as Ms. Yingluck must stick to her promises over reconciliation, so she will have to find a way to defer many of her campaign promises to spend. These pledges helped secure her victory, but they are unaffordable. For instance, she proposed a rise of the minimum wage, to 300 baht ($10) a day. That would be hideously costly for the country, especially for small businesses in precisely the poorer regions that Thaksinites claim to embrace. The Democrats had some better ideas, for instance, varying the minimum wage according to regional pay levels, Ms. Yingluck should ditch her plans and embrace theirs.

It will be an early test of whether she will pursue sensible policies rather than populist ones. It will also be an indication of whether this unusual new prime minister really is the person to return Thailand to a steady path forward.[347]

---

346 *Bangkok Post*, "Yingluck, Abhisit endorsed by EC," July 19, 2011.
347 *The Economist*, "Thailand's Election: A Precious chance," July 9, 2011, pp. 14 & 23.

Royal Decree Endorsement

Following the Election Commission's endorsement of 496 MPs, which exceeds the legal required minimum of 475 MPs of the total of 500 needed for the House to convene, His Majesty the King on Friday the 29th of July authorized the opening of the assembly of parliament. Former House Speaker Chai Chidchob, as the senior most MP will temporarily act as speaker until the first House meeting selects the new Speaker. Several candidates have appeared, however, the most likely is Khon Kaen MP Somsak Kiatsuranont, who has kept his distance from the red-shirts and therefore would be less likely a target of the opposition.[348]

As of August 4, 2011 all 500 MPs had received their documents certifying their status. A recount in constituency 2 of Yala province proved Mr. Abdulkarim Dengrakina had received 530 votes more than his nearest rival, Sukarno Matha of the Puea Thai party, on Sunday. He was the last MP certified.[349]

Prime Minister-elect Yingluck Shinawatra said her cabinet is 80 percent complete and will be finalized in a day or two and forwarded to His Majesty the King for his endorsement. She said the cabinet will contain four non-MPs. She said she would try to ensure there were cabinet ministers from all regions of the country because they were the people who best understood the people's problems.[350]

On Thursday, August 10, 2011, Ms. Yingluck led her cabinet ministers to take the oath of allegiance before His Majesty the King at Siriraj Hospital. The King reiterated the importance of honesty to ensure the country's peace, prosperity and the people's well-being.[351]

---

348 *Bangkok Post*, "His Majesty endorses parliament asssembly," July 30, 2011.
349 *Bangkok Post*, "All 500 MPs have ratification papers," August 4, 2011.
350 *Bangkok Post*, "Yingluck: Four outsiders will be in cabinet," August 8, 2011.
351 *Bangkok Post*, "King urges govt to ensure peace," August 10, 2011.

Conclusions on the Struggle for Democracy in Thailand

Democracy as Abraham Lincoln would have defined it was *government of the people, by the people and for the people.* So as we look to Asia and particularly to Thailand in this paper, how are they succeeding in achieving democracy.

The Student Revolution of 38 years ago, launched a populist uprising that was repeatedly crushed, and yet survived to the real growth in 1992. The Democrat Party of central and southern Thailand assumed the mantel of leadership in the 1990s and they were challenged by the north and northeast regions under Thaksin's astute leadership in 2001 until his personality revealed itself in the sale of his Shin Corporation (Broadcast Media) and the **brutality** in the Muslim conflict in south Thailand.

The Coup of 2006 and the Constitution of 2007 which was ratified by popular referendum, clearly showed Bangkok concurrence; the acts which transpired thereafter led first by the Yellow-shirted royalists with demonstrations and the airport take-overs, were followed by the Red-shirts and their two-month rally in Bangkok, revealed an unwillingness to acknowledge the rights of rural Thais to participate in governance.

The failure of the police to participate in mob conrol until nearly the end of the Red-shirted rally reveals another dimension of Thai society: namely, the role of classmate loyalty, even stronger than national allegiance! Prime Minister Abhisit has created a Police Reform Panel and it will only succeed if he leads with total endorsement!

The need for an open and participatory election to bring about a government of the people, by the people and for the people to allow social changes to occur with a parliamentary structure has now been completed. It has been endorsed by His Majesty the King and not challenged by the Courts, such that we may now see peaceful and evolutionary government in Thailand.

Prime Minister Yingluck Shinawatra is politically inexperienced, with a career spanning only about 80 days. However, she earned a degree in Public Administration from Chiang Mai University and went on to Kentucky State University to earn a master's degree also in Public Administration. She then took that education and applied it in the family businesses for more than twenty years. Yingluck has demonstrated the criteria for leadership that Thaksin cited as essentials for being the new Prime minister for Thailand.

How Disaster is Contributing to Reconciliation.

The floods that ravaged the factory systems in the Central Plains were a fifty or one-hundred year storm event it is generally agreed. Prime Minister Yingluck Shinawatra together with her Strategic Formulation Committee for Water Resource Management are working diligently to design modernizations to the water flow from North Thailand to the sea.

On February 25th His Majesty the King granted an audience to this Committee and the Prime Minister at Siriraj Hospital. Here we see the King meeting the Committee:

His Majesty the King is widely recognized as an expert on water and flood management. He expressed concern about deforestation and the resultant flooding and urged the government to take severe action against those responsible. His Majesty advised cultivating mixed forest of both fast-growing and slow-growing tree species. He pointed out that slow-growing trees put deep roots into the ground helping to prevent landslides.

The Committee has assigned the Royal Irrigation Department the task of finding measures to speed up the drainage of water from the Chao Phraya River in Nakon Sawan to the sea Two options are appearing: I) improving existing canals and 2) creating new canals to increase water flow capacity. The new canals would divert water from the Chao Phraya to the Tha Chin River in the west and the Pa Sak and Bang Pakong Rivers in the east.[352]

---

352 *Bangkok Post,* King meets PM and Strategic Formulation Committee at Sirirat Hospital, Feb. 26, 2012.

Index

A

A Look at the Need for Steel 61
Abac Poll of May 2, 2011 173
Abattoir 15
Abhisit Vejjajiva, Democrat Party leader expresses Concern 124
Abhisit Vejjajiva, Prime Minister 89, 106, 124, 129, 131, 133, 142, 143, 149, 156, 158, 159, 171, 172, 179, 180, 183
Acheson, Dean G., "Crisis in China" 30
Adjusting the Economy After the Crash 52
All things Considered – Thailand's New Order 49
American Club 5, 6
Amnat Gekhuntod, "community savior" 113
Ancient Law of King Mangrai 114
Anupong Paochinda, Army Chief 140
Apirak Kosayodhin, Governor of Bangkok 112
Army and Tak Bai rioters 102, 182
ASHA, (USAID) 68, 69
Assets Scrutiny Committee 101
Ayer, Dr. Frederic L. 13, 17, 40, 58, 62

B

Bangkok Christian College 11
BBC televises the debate 181
BCC – Bangkok Christian College (K-12) 1, 12
Bodin, Jean, *Books of the Commonweale* 3

Boonyaratkalin, Sonthi (Army C-in-C) 94, 102, 119, 123, 157
Bridges 82, 108
Britain negotiates with Communist China 72
BRL – Business Research Co., Ltd. 13, 58, 81
Brohm, Dr. John, IIE 7
Burma 18, 60, 80, 82, 114, 160, 161
Butwell, Dr. Richard on Burma 18

C

Cambodia's Khao Preah Vihear Temple 29, 33, 167
Center for the Resolution of the Emergency Situation (CRES) 147, 148, 149
Chairman Mao 13, 49
Chaiwut Bannawat, Ministry of Industry 160
Chamlong Srimuang, Maj. Gen. (PAD "yellow-shirt" leader) 79, 127, 139, 167
Chatchai Choonhavan (former PM) 95
Chatrabote, Rev. Mr. Maetri 56
Chavarat Charnvirakul, Interior Minister 132, 133
Chiang Mai 7, 8, 16, 45, 55, 56, 63, 64, 65, 68, 69, 70, 101, 129, 172, 189
Chiang Saen port in Chiang Rai province 107
Chicago & Bangkok had Similarities 11, 12
Chief Court Brahmin 136
China and India sign Treaty with ASEAN 90

Chinese Dams on the Mekong River 107, 108, 161
Chokchai Building 12
Chuan Leekpai 153
Clark Air Force Base, Philippines 10
Classmate Loyalty 155, 188
Constitutional Court 52, 95, 129, 131
Constitution Drafting 53, 119, 120, 121, 122, 123
Constitution Drafting Assembly (CDA) 120, 121, 122, 123
Constitution Referendum August 19, 2007 wins Endorsement 121, 123
Corn Syrup 61
Corporate Governance/Best Listed Firms 92
Council for Democratic Reform (CDR) 95, 96
Council for Democratic Reform under the Monarchy (CDRM) 94
Covington & Burling 2, 29, 33
Creating Community 47
Criminal Court releases eight Red-Shirts 176
Criteria for Leadership 177, 189
cultural boundary 87, 89
CVT – Christian Volunteer in Thailand 1

D

Day, Jess 8
Dellen, Dr. Joseph 10
Democrat Party 77, 89, 101, 105, 106, 124, 127, 129, 141, 144, 153, 154, 159, 170, 171, 172, 174, 176, 180, 184, 188
Democrat Party Launches Thailand Reform Plan 171
Democrats Offer Amnesty Plan 174
Democrats Seek P.T. Dissolution 184
DETRI 18
DOE, BR-Bureau of Reclamation 21, 22, 23
Don Muang Airport 5
Doran, Dr. Kenneth D. 8
DOW Chemical Co. 106
Drainage Tunnels 12, 59, 60, 112, 113, 159, 160
Dr. Paul Lauby, UBCHEA, New York 65, 66, 67, 68
DSI seeks 20 new warrants for terrorism 152
Dusit Thani Hotel 12

E

ECAFE – United Nations, Economic Commission For Asia and the Far East 15
Economic and Technical Assistance Treaty 33
1997 Economic Crisis 72, 73
EGAT (Electric Generating Authority of Thailand) 18, 20, 27, 28, 80, 81, 104, 105, 161, 162
Ehrensberger, Dr. Ray 10, 55, 56
Election Commission 51, 121, 141, 172, 179, 184, 185, 187
Election Commission Acts 185
Elliott, William Y. 2, 66
Esso Standard Thailand, Ltd. 17
Ethic of politeness 6

F

Field Marshals Thonom and Praphat 57, 97
Finance and Property Restructuring 92
Finer, Samuel E. 66
Firestone Tyre & Rubber Co., (Thailand) Ltd. 15
Fresh Water for a Growing City 59
Fulbright Education Treaty 33
Funding the University's Development 65

G

General Motors Corporation 58
Guatemala Corn 61
Gulf of Tonkin 3

H

Hambali capture 87, 88
Hamlin, Dr. E. John 7, 55
Hankins, JoAnne 7
Hard currency floats 73
Harvard University 2, 70, 87
Heavy work 10
His Majesty the King dissolves the House May 10, 2011 172, 179
His Majesty the King endorsed Cabinet on August 10, 2011 187
"How are you," in Asia is "Have you eaten yet?" 36
How Do You Clean Up Corruption 51
Hu Jintao, China President 108, 110, 136
Hunsberger, Dr. Warren 18

I

IBRD (International Bank for Reconstruction and Development) 20, 21, 22, 25, 26, 27, 29, 84
Industry/Steel and Investments 111
Infant Food Study 63
Infrastructure Needs 161
Inouye, Sen. Daniel K. 68
Institute for the Study of Religion and Culture 70
International Air Transport Association 130
International Court of Justice 167, 168
International Executive Service Corps 16
International Institute for Management Development 90
Investment flows 91
IRAQ 66, 88, 112
ISB – International School of Bangkok 7, 8, 9, 10, 11, 12, 13, 22, 57, 58
Italian-Thai Development Plc. (ITD) 160
"It's a Landslide!" 183

J

Japanese investments 91
Jatuporn Prompan, UDD "Red-shirt leader" 140, 147, 152, 164, 176
Johnson, President Lyndon B. 3
Jorgenson & Jorgenson 6
JP Morgan Chase & Co. 132

K

Kair Fai, *weir dam* manager 114
Kambhu, M.L.Xujati 21, 26, 27
Kasit Piromya, Foreign Minister 132, 168
Khao Phra Vihar 2, 29, 33, 167
Khattiya Sawasdipol, Maj.-Gen. "Seh Daeng" 140, 144, 146
King Bhumibol Adilyadej 95, 100, 101, 113, 120, 127, 135, 136, 156, 178
Kingshill, Dr. Konrad 7, 68
Klongs 12, 59
Klong Toey 16, 59, 150
KMT Chinese 72
Kofi Annan, UN Sec.-Gen. 135, 136
Korn Chatokavanij economist and Finance Minister 132, 133, 138
Kramer, Dr. Carlisle 9, 10
Krue Sae Mosque and Tak Bai 102, 182

L

Ladd, D. Milton 68
Landon, Kenneth P. 4, 18, 45
LeFever, Ernest W. 3

Linne Tholin, Engineer 12, 42, 59, 60, 65, 84, 112

M

Mabbett, Dr. Joseph 10, 11, 55
MacArthur, General Douglas 30, 31
MACTHAI 10, 13, 55
Mae Khao Campus 69
Malik, Yakov A. 31
Marlow, Shelton 9
Martial law 53, 56, 57
Maryland University (FED) 13, 55, 56
McDaniel, Charlotte 7
McDaniel, Dr. Edwin B. 8
Mendota Research of New Jersey 5
Military Assistance Treaty with Thailand 21, 33, 37
Milk firms pool resources 85
MK – mission kid 1
Monsoon Drainage systems 59
Montesquieu, Baron Charles, *Spirit of the Laws* 3
MR Sukumbhand 151

N

Nam Theun 2 Dam (Laos) 80, 81
NaRanong, Dr. Lydia (Dan) on Thailand 18
National Food Institute (NFI) 107
National Legislative Assembly 97, 116, 119
National Peace-Keeping Council (NPKC) 95
Need for Truth and Reconciliation 164
NGO (Non-Governmental Organization) 50, 74
Niebuhr, H. Richard, *Christ and Culture* 49, 70
Nimmanhaeminda, Dr. Sukich 56, 64
Noranit Setabutr, CDA Chair 123
NPA Grand Sale 92

NPL – Non-Performing Loans 44, 73

O

Oxford University 65, 66, 68

P

PAD asks EC to Dissolve P.T. Party 174
Pakistan Water Delegation 2
Panitan Wattanayakorn, government spokesman 148
Participant Training Inventory 40
Payap College Opens Its Doors 63
People Power 50
People's Alliance for Democracy (PAD) 79, 127, 128, 129, 130, 131, 139, 143, 158, 164, 167, 170, 173, 174
People's Power Party (PPP) 125, 129, 158
Pick-up trucks 59, 109
Pilings (27 meters long) 12
ping-pong diplomacy 13
Piyaoui, Thanpuying Chanut 12
Port of Bangkok at Klong Toey 16
PPT Exploration and Production Plc 86
Prasong Soonsiri, Sqn-Ldr. Chair of CDC 120, 123
Prem Tinsulanonda 79, 96, 102
Prem Tinsulanonda, Privy Council president 79, 96, 102
Prime Minister Yingluck Shinawatra 52, 53, 74, 75, 77, 78, 87, 94, 95, 96, 102, 120, 124, 127, 129, 133, 138, 140, 148, 149, 152, 153, 154, 157, 170, 174, 177, 178, 179, 182, 183, 184, 185, 186, 187, 188
Prince Royal's College, Chiang Mai 7, 8, 16, 45, 55, 56, 63, 64, 65, 68, 69, 70, 101, 129, 172, 189
Proposed subway lines 60, 84
Puea Thai Party 133, 138, 152, 159,

174, 175, 177, 178, 179, 184, 185, 187
Puea Thai Party lodges complaint with EC 179, 184
Put a Tiger in Your Tank 17

R

Ratchaprasong intersection 141, 148, 173, 176, 180
Red-shirt Rally promised Peaceful 175
"Religion and Culture" Conference 70
RID – Royal Irrigation Department 23, 114
Riggs, Fred Warren, "prismatic society" 23, 47, 97, 119, 157
Robinson, Edgar 5
Rotary Club luncheon 90
Roth, Harold H. 1, 2
Ruyffelaere, Col. Rayond F. 55
Ryburn, Rev. Dr. Horace 7, 65

S

Salween River Dam 80
Samak Sundaravej, initiates Thai nurse training for Bahrain 117, 125, 126
Samart Chokkanapitak, RID Chief 113
Sam Houston State University 100
Samut Sakhon Province Coal-Mining Conflicts 105, 165
Sanitsuda Ekachai, B.P. Associate Editor 128, 134, 163, 164
Sanpasit Viriyasiri, legendary newsman 128
Sattahip 16
Seventh Day Adventist Hospital 6
Shin Corporation sale 78, 138, 139, 154, 157, 188
Shrimp production 85
Siam Kraft Paper Co., Ltd. 17
Siamwalla, Dr. Ammar 90, 116

Silliman University 66, 68
Silom/Sala Daeng area 142
Sirindhorn Learning Resource Center 69
Skytrain 82
Society Structure 98
Soft-Power 4
Somchai Wongsawat, PM and brother-in-law of Thaksin 128, 129, 131, 185
Somkid Lertphaithoon, Thammasat University Faculty Dean 141
Sondhi Limthongkul 78, 79, 127, 139
Songkhram, Field Marshal Pibul 31
Southeast Asian Treaty Organization (SEATO) 33
Southern Thailand Arena of Conflict 182
Southwest University (Chongqing, China) 64
Squatters 56, 57
Stanton, Edwin F. 20, 21
Starbucks 151
Straits of Malacca 32
Streeten, Paul P. 66, 67
Studies on Thailand's Market Potential 13, 15
Superior brown rice 85
Surayud Chulanont, Privy Councillor and General 96, 100, 102, 115, 116
Surichai Wankaew, Chulalongkorn University 141

T

Tall buildings 12, 163
Tata Steel 90, 91
Teachers under threat 89
Thai Airport Ground Services wins Mideast Contracts 112
Thai Bureaucracy 45, 46, 50, 60, 79, 123, 124, 135
Thai Hua Rubber Co. 86

Thailand and China Open Linkage Discussions 108
THAILAND: An On-Going Struggle for Democracy 138
Thailand plunges in global ratings 90
Thailand's General Election 182
Thailand's IT Potential, winner of "Imagine Cup" 117
Thailand's Supreme Court Confiscates B46.37bn from Thaksin 138
Thailand, the Crisis Leader 42
Thailand Theological Seminary 7, 55, 64
Thai Petrochemical Industries (TPI, now IRPC) 106
Thai Rak Thai Party 74, 86, 94, 96, 101, 184
Thai troops to Iraq 88
Thaksin Shinawatra 52, 53, 74, 77, 87, 94, 95, 96, 102, 120, 124, 127, 129, 133, 138, 140, 148, 149, 152, 153, 154, 157, 170, 174, 177, 178, 179, 182, 184, 185
Thammarak Isarangkura Na Ayudhaya, Defense Minister 102
The *human touch* 180
The Leaders of PAD and UDD 139
The USOM-Thailand Contract 61
This Mysterious Oneness 48
Thongnak Sawekchinda 165
Thrayuth Boonmi 74
Three-legged Stool 18
Tocqueville, Alexis de, Democracy in America 3
Tolerance of Controversy 45
Tormenting Issues Afflicting Thai Society 166
Trained Participants by Field of Training 40, 66
Trans-Peninsula Oil Pipeline 103

U

Udon Thani Provincial Court 151, 158
Unger, Ambassador Leonard 57
United Front of Democracy Against Dictatorship (UDD) 128, 133, 139, 140, 141, 143, 147, 149, 158, 162, 164, 170, 174, 176, 178, 186
United nations Office on Drugs and Crime (UNODC) 100
United Stevedoring Co., Ltd. 16
Urgent Need for Land Reforms 163
USOM-Thailand 21, 29, 33, 61, 62, 79

V

Valves, and more Valves 62
Vandenbosch, Amry, Thailand, the Test Case 4, 6, 32, 33
Vasit Dejkunchorn, Police General, reform cmte chairman 154
Veera Somkhwamkid, TPN Coordinator for PAD 167
Virginia Quarterly Review 4, 31, 49
Viya Crab Produccts Co. 86
VOMPOT 18, 53, 57

W

Wat pathumwanaram 153
Wattana Wittaya Academy (K-12) 6
Who was Coup'ed? 119
"Will you give his youngest sister a chance?" 181
World Heritage Committee 167, 168
"World's Kitchen" 85

X

Xishuangbanna Gas & Petroleum 106

Y

Yanhee Dam 5, 11, 28
YINGLUCK SHINAWATRA 52,
　　53, 74, 75, 77, 78, 87, 94, 95, 96,
　　102, 120, 124, 127, 129, 133,
　　138, 140, 148, 149, 152, 153, 154,
　　157, 170, 174, 177, 178, 179, 182,
　　183, 184, 185, 186, 187, 188
YMCA on Sathorn Tai Road 56
Young, Sen. Milton 68

Z

Zimmerman, Dr. Robert 47, 61, 63

CPSIA information can be obtained at www.ICGtesting.com
Printed in the USA
BVOW041002180612

292964BV00001B/2/P